SERIES EDITOR: LEE JOHNSON

OSPREY MILITARY MEN-AT-ARMS 300

FRENCH FOREIGN LEGION

INFANTRY AND CAVALRY SINCE 1945

TEXT BY
MARTIN WINDROW

COLOUR PLATES BY
MIKE CHAPPELL

First published in Great Britain in 1996 by Osprey, an imprint of Reed Consumer Books Limited, Michelin House, 81 Fulham Road, London SW3 6RB and Auckland, Melbourne, Singapore and Toronto

Reprinted 1997

Osprey
2nd Floor, Unit 6, Spring Gardens, Tinworth Street, Vauxhall, London SE11 5EH

ISBN 1 85532 621 3

Filmset in Great Britain by KDI, Newton le Willows
Printed through World Print Ltd., Hong Kong

Editor: Sharon van der Merwe
Design: the Black Spot

For a catalogue of all books published by Osprey Military please write to:
The Marketing Manager, Osprey Publishing Ltd., Michelin House,
81 Fulham Road, London SW3 6RB

Author's note

This book should be read as complementary to Elite 6 *French Foreign Legion Paratroops*; certain basic information found in that title has not been repeated here for space reasons.

French unit titles, etc., have not been italicised in this text. A slightly different convention is adopted in the commentaries on the colour plates and is explained at the beginning of that section. Real consistency in the spellings of Indochinese and North African place names has proved impossible when working from a number of French and English-language sources, and is not claimed here.

The author wishes to thank all those who assisted during the preparation of this book, wittingly or unwittingly, and particularly Wayne Braby, Simon Dunstan, Simon Forty, Eric Morgan, Carl Schulze, Ron Volstad and Jim Worden. A further reading list will be found at the end of the main text.

Publisher's Note

Readers may wish to study this title in conjunction with the following Osprey publications:

Elite 6 *French Foreign Legion Paratroops*

Artist's Note

Readers may care to note that the original paintings from which the colour plates in this book were prepared are available for private sale. All reproduction copyright whatsoever is retained by the publisher. All enquiries should be addressed to:

Mike Chappell, 14 Downlands, Walmer, Deal, Kent CT14 7XA

The publishers regret that they can enter into no correspondence upon this matter.

FRENCH FOREIGN LEGION

THE LEGION IN 1945

May 1945 found three units of the legendary French Foreign Legion among the victorious Allied armies in the West. Only one – the 13e Demi-Brigade – had rallied to De Gaulle's Free French forces in 1940 after Narvik, fighting in East and North Africa, Italy and Alsace. After the Allied invasion of French North Africa in late 1942, France's Armée d'Afrique was reorganised to provide several divisions based on current US models, and equipped by the US Army. The Legion's 1er, 2e, 3e, 4e, and (disbanded) 6e Régiments Étrangers d'Infanterie provided men for a new three-battalion Régiment de Marche de la Légion Étrangère. The RMLE provided the mechanised infantry for the new 5e Division Blindé; and the 1er Régiment Étranger de Cavalerie served as the division's reconnaissance regiment. The REC and RMLE saw hard fighting in Alsace in the last winter of the war, and by May 1945 they were deep inside southern Germany and Austria.

Politically traumatised; fought over at ruinous cost during her liberation; her economy and administration in tatters; her people engaged in a bloody internecine settling of accounts; her army, a confused mixture of French and colonial native troops engaged under widely

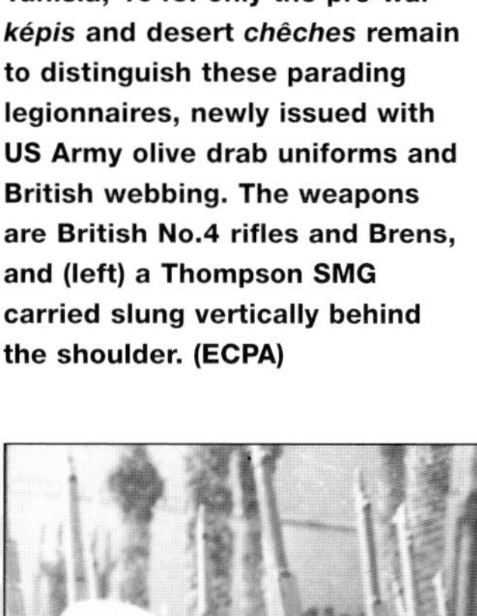

Tunisia, 1943: only the pre-war *képis* and desert *chêches* remain to distinguish these parading legionnaires, newly issued with US Army olive drab uniforms and British webbing. The weapons are British No.4 rifles and Brens, and (left) a Thompson SMG carried slung vertically behind the shoulder. (ECPA)

The pre-war French sand-khaki shirt and shorts, authorised as everyday uniform in tropical garrisons in 1937; by 1945 stocks were low and they were more often replaced by British and American khaki drill clothing until the new French long-sleeved shirt and slacks became generally available at the end of the 1940s. This group, wearing the shirt and shorts with puttees and boots or sandals, were photographed at Christmas 1941 serving with the Motorised Company of the 4e REI at Foum-el-Hassan in southern Morocco. Note the taller model of *képi* authorised in 1935 for re-enlisted *sous-officiers*. (Courtesy Charles Milassin)

differing terms of service, and primarily committed to her occupation zone in Germany – France in 1945 was in no condition to mount major colonial expeditionary forces. In her most prestigious colony the power vacuum of 1945 would prove costly.

INDOCHINA 1946-54

Indochina – modern north, central and south Vietnam (then, Tonkin, Annam and Cochinchina respectively) – had been ruled by the occupying French, together with Laos and Cambodia, either directly or under the polite fiction of various protocols and treaties, since the 1880s. By the 1920s, a posting East was regarded by French colonial troops as the prized reward for long service and good conduct. It offered comfortable barracks, beautiful scenery, a relaxed pace of duty, charming female company, and servants to carry out the menial fatigues – servants whose wages were within the means of even a common légionnaire, on a scale of local pay and allowances which could total five times what he had received in Morocco.

A first taste of bitter change came in 1930-32, when partly Communist-led risings in Tonkin and northern Annam were crushed with some brutality, leaving insurgent leaders on the run but with valuable propaganda for future recruitment. Between 1942 and 1945 the Vichy government was obliged to tolerate Japanese garrisons being planted in Indochina. The French troops were forced to sit out the war; meanwhile the local Communists revived and expanded their clandestine network. In March 1945 the Japanese attacked the French garrisons without warning. Survivors of the Legion's 5^{e} REI formed the

Annam, 1946: a post garrison of the 2e REI clown for the camera with the locals. They wear mostly British KD, and carry Brens, No.4 rifles and a Sten. Note the bamboo walls of the post – most of these isolated garrisons of 60-80 men had defences more suitable to a 19th-century police post, with earth and timber walls, buildings of (at best) flimsy local brick, sandbag blockhouses with marginal overhead cover, and inadequate barbed wiring usually supplemented by sharpened bamboo *chevaux-de-frise*. (Courtesy Charles Milassin)

bulk of a column which managed to fight its way north into Nationalist China. The subsequent Japanese surrender was taken by the Chinese in the north and by a British force in the south.

The leaders of the Communist underground – Ho Chi Minh and his lieutenants, including the militarily brilliant Vo Nguyen Giap – seized every opportunity to extend their grip. Their 'Viet Minh' guerrilla force would number more than 50,000 by the end of 1946, supported by regional militias, and by a widespread logistic and intelligence infrastructure among the population. In September 1945 Ho declared the

Foreign Legion Unit Designations

BATAILLON
Battalion strength and organisation varied during this period. In Indochina the norm was an HQ element, four rifle companies, and often a locally-recruited auxiliary company. Support weapons were usually insufficient to form a separate company, being grouped under the HQ element. Companies were numbered consecutively throughout the regiment, e.g. 1er-4e Cies. in I Bn., 5e-8e Cies. in II Bn., etc.

In Algeria from c.1956 the large single-battalion mobile intervention regiments were commonly divided into an HQ & Services company; two 'groups' each with a tactical HQ and three rifle companies; a support company, or a support & recce company with a small integral armoured car element.

CCS Compagnie de Commandement et Services
(HQ & Services Company)

CEA Compagnie d'Éclairage et Appui
(Recce & Support Company)

Compagnie Portée/Escadron Porté
Motorised infantry company/squadron

Demi-Brigade ('Half-brigade')
Traditional alternative title for battalion- or regiment-sized unit, retained for historic reasons by 13e Demi-Brigade de la Légion Étrangère (13e DBLE).

RÉGIMENT
During 1945-c.1956 Foreign Legion regiments normally consisted of two or more *bataillons* or *groupes d'escadrons* serving separately. From about that date they were normally reduced to single-battalion strength (see *Bataillon* above).
Since 1962 regimental strength has varied (see details in body text).

RE Régiment Étranger
'Foreign Regiment'
Legion unit with other than combat role.

REC Régiment Étranger de Cavalerie
'Foreign Cavalry Regiment'

REG Régiment Étranger de Génie
'Foreign Engineer Regiment'

REI Régiment Étranger d'Infanterie
'Foreign Infantry Regiment'
Title style for Legion combat units.

Régiment de Marche (Also Bataillon de Marche.)
A temporary 'marching' or task force unit usually assembled from men of more than one of the Legion's historic numbered regiments.

'Democratic Republic of Vietnam' from Hanoi. The Viet Minh ruthlessly eliminated all dissent, while posing to the Allies as democratic patriots seeking self-determination.

When the French finally managed to send an expeditionary corps of some 56,000 men to Indochina in early 1946 they were still stinging from the humiliations of 1940-45 and in no mood for compromise. Even moderate Vietnamese leaders, alert to matters of 'face', had seen French troops driven out by fellow Asians, and were not about to accept the *status quo ante bellum.* The powder keg was duly detonated by the 'Haiphong Incident' of 20 November 1946, bringing negotiations to a bloody end. Ho Chi Minh and Giap took the Viet Minh main force back to their sanctuaries in the jungle hills of Tonkin; and began what still provides historians with a perfect text-book example of the practice of Maoist guerrilla warfare. The non-Communist traditional leadership class were devious and self-seeking allies for the French; the mass of peasantry bent with whichever wind blew them, trying merely to survive, as the powerless have done since the dawn of time.

The enemy and the terrain

The Viet Minh leadership survived, narrowly, the first French airborne strike at their main refuges – the 'Viet Bac' – in the High Region north of the Red River Delta around Hanoi. (Later French operations would occasionally destroy supply dumps and secret factories, but these successes, achieved by disproportionate effort, were never more than temporary.) The Viet Minh steadily expanded their grip all over the country, emerging to fight only on ground and at times of their choosing.

Sidi-bel-Abbes, December 1947: a company of the 1er REI display a motley collection of pre-war French leather equipment and tunics (very few of them with the new sleeve *écusson*, but all with *epaulettes de tradition*), US Army trousers and leggings, and old Lebel rifles. The senior NCO or warrant officer in the foreground wears British battledress, the officer French pre-war service dress. (Courtesy Wayne Braby)

Between 1947 and 1950 Giap concentrated on building up his VM main force in the hills of Tonkin, while harassing the French all over Vietnam. In Cochinchina and Annam most of the fighting was done by regional forces supported by militia; the main force or *Chuc luc* seldom sent units far from its northern bases, and proved extremely elusive. The French were denied their hope for a quick victory – and their best officers recognised that they did not have the men or the resources for a long war to which, for legal reasons, French conscripts could not be committed. Not all their generals (nor their ministers, during a period of chaotic political instability in France, where this '*sale guerre*' was widely unpopular) were as clear-thinking.

The Viet Minh maintained a constant campaign of guerrilla pin-pricks. A remote post would fall silent, to be found ruined and empty when the relief column, thinned by booby-traps and exhausted by bypassing blown bridges, finally arrived. A convoy would be expertly ambushed in a mountain gorge, the scores of corpses stripped of every weapon and every round before the attackers melted away. A village headman would be persuaded to supply rice and carrying-parties – or would be found gaudily butchered, as a lesson to the hesitant. Everywhere, every night of the war, roads would be cleverly booby-trapped, or cut by dozens of interlocking 'piano key' ditches; every morning long-suffering road-opening patrols would straggle out once more – and straggle back, with one of their number silent and bloody in a slung poncho, or crippled by *punji*-stakes.

The losses mounted steadily; in two years in the relatively quiet south the 2^{e} REI suffered 200 casualties. Some French commanders persisted in regarding the Viets as little more than colonial bandits; but from the start the French only truly controlled their main towns and posts, and some stretches of the major roads during daylight. Surprise was impossible; and nothing seemed to work. Frustration and fear provoked brutalities against the civil population which became routine, thus increasing the insurgents' base of support.

The varying terrain – thinly inhabited, thickly wooded mountains in northern Tonkin and the highlands of central Annam; a fringe of thickly populated rice country along the coast; jungle and swamp in the southern wetlands of Cochinchina and in the major river deltas – favoured the elusive and enduring Viet Minh. The roads were few and vulnerable; the VM became expert at luring rescue columns along predictable routes, only to destroy them in their turn. The terrain limited the mobility of the French mechanised units, while the VM proved adept at camouflage and night movement, avoiding the attentions of the French air force; in both these assets, and in airlift capacity, the French were in any case always far too weak for decisive success.

The conventional wisdom was that if the Viets would only come out of the hills and swamps in force they could be destroyed. Giap avoided any such confrontation while he patiently built, equipped and trained the Soviet-style regiments of the *Chuc luc*. French intelligence was poor throughout the war, and the high command consistently underestimated the numbers and quality of their enemy.

By 1950 Giap's main force would total perhaps 100,000 men, typically organised in numbered four-battalion regiments, plentifully equipped with World War II small arms and machine guns and with some mortars

Tonkin, 1951: the concrete tower of a Legion-held post in the De Lattre Line displays battle damage from a night attack. By this date construction and materials gave better protection against mortar and bazooka fire; the blockhouses were usually armed with Browning .50 cal. or .30 cal. machine guns (US aid began to flow much faster after the outbreak of the Korean War). Most posts had either an artillery piece or a mortar or two in open pits inside the walls. (Courtesy Wayne Braby)

and even light artillery, of Russian, Chinese, Japanese and French origin. These manoeuvre units were backed by about twice as many regional guerrillas who could be called out at local need. The Communist victory in China at the end of 1949, and early Communist victories in Korea the following summer, would improve this force dramatically.

The Foreign Legion in Indochina

Against this enemy the French Far East Expeditionary Corps (CEFEO) could muster, at various dates, between 115,000 and 235,000 men, though far fewer were available for combat operations. The largest proportion – 50,000-100,000 – were locally recruited, lightly equipped, usually immobile and of limited value. About 50,000 were French volunteers in Colonial or Metropolitan infantry, artillery, airborne and armoured units. North and West African colonies provided some 25,000, mostly infantry; by 1952-54 their morale was often, though not invariably, suspect. In March 1952, at peak strength, the Foreign Legion had some 20,000 men in-country: about 13,000 in four infantry regiments; 1,800 plus the same number of attached local infantry in one armoured/amphibious cavalry regiment; 1,400 paratroopers; and some 4,000 technical troops. They represented the largest European infantry element and, at that date, about 8 per cent of the CEFEO. During the first half of the war the 13^{e} DBLE was based in the wetlands of Cochinchina, most of the 2^{e} REI in Annam, the 5^{e} REI in the Red River

Cochinchina, October 1950: US M29C Weasels (in French usage, 'Crabs') of the 1er REC's 1er Groupe d'Escadrons cross a waterway during an operation near Tra Vinh. The waterlogged million-acre wilderness of the Plain of Reeds started just 25km west of Saigon, offering the regional Viet Minh limitless cover. Each of the three squadrons of the 1er GE had three platoons of six M29s. (ECPA)

Tonkin, May 1952: during Operation Dromadaire near Hung Yen, a 1er REC trooper of the 2e Groupement Autonome mans the .30 cal. on his Crab. The M29C was never designed as a combat vehicle, but the Legion fitted them all with .30 cals. or LMGs, and those of support elements with 57mm recoilless rifles. (ECPA)

Delta, the 3e REI in northern Tonkin closest to the Chinese border, and the 1er REC dispersed throughout the country. After 1950 the bulk of the Legion infantry would be concentrated in Tonkin.

The Legion's total strength rose in 1945-50 from some 14,000 to about 30,000 men. Cut off from its traditional sources of recruits during World War II, the Legion fell hungrily upon the POW and Displaced Persons camps of Europe where the human flotsam of a whole continent had been washed up by the tide of world war. The regiments which remained in North Africa – the 1er, 4e and re-formed 6e REI and the 2e REC – became little more than basic training, depot and transit units for the Expeditionary Corps. (Perhaps half the légionnaires in Indochina were Germans; the popular legend of 'Waffen-SS veterans' has been enormously exaggerated, however.)

Nevertheless, the Legion suffered the same shortage of effective manpower as the CEFEO as a whole. Indochina killed French junior officers literally as fast as St Cyr could graduate them; and the plethora of non-white units constantly drained away officers and NCOs for cadres. The lack of experienced junior leaders became chronic; in early 1951, for instance, the four-battalion 5e REI was short by 52 warrant officers and 71 *sergents-chef*. It became commonplace for battalions in the neglected south to be reduced to one officer per company, throwing ever greater burdens on young NCOs who often had no time to grow into the job.

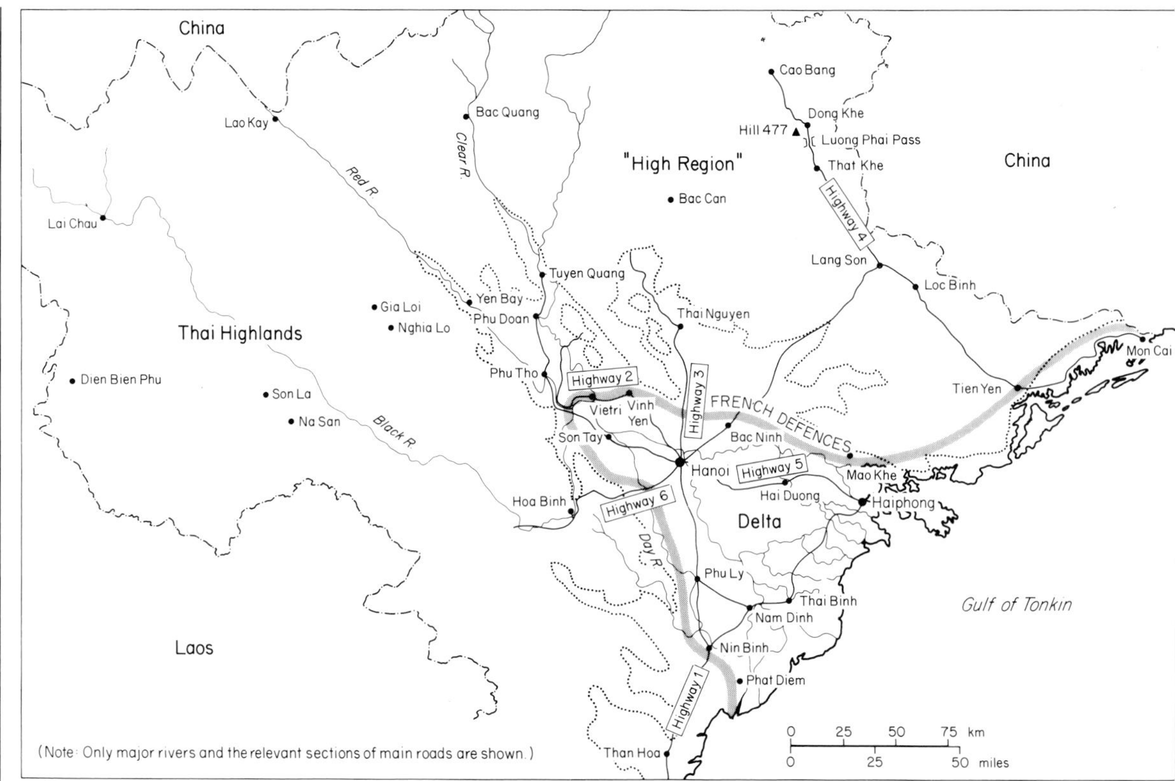

Simplified map of Tonkin, the cockpit of the Indochina War; Giap's highland strongholds were in the 'Viet Bac' around Bac Can, and from early 1950 he formed and trained his new divisions in camps immediately over the Chinese border from the line of posts along Highway 4. (RC)

Many early enlistees left after their first five-year contract, and the increased tempo of fighting and casualties in 1950-54 coincided with a relative shortage of replacements; those who did arrive were sent to the manoeuvre battalions in Tonkin, so the units in Cochinchina and Annam suffered worst of all. Enlistees in the second half of the war were noticeably younger and included fewer World War II veterans, and the CEFEO's hunger for replacements denied them more than fairly sketchy training.

The Legion's rough-and-ready methods, and careful indoctrination with the traditions of the corps, succeeded to the degree that Legion units could be counted upon to fight with stubborn courage, especially in defence; but the wide dispersal of units in 'penny packets' which characterised the first years of the war prevented much battalion training, and later there was no time for it. Again, the inadequacy of the French mobile reserve coupled with Giap's growing ability to achieve local superiority first in one sector, then in another, led to constant movement of French units, often into areas of completely different terrain than that which they had learned to master.

The 1951 Reforms 'Le jaunissement', and the Groupes Mobiles

The RC.4 disaster of October 1950 (see below) brought out an energetic if short-lived new governor-general, Gen. de Lattre de Tassigny. The Red River Delta around Hanoi and Haiphong – the vital French heartland – was now protected against infiltration and attack by a tight belt of more than 900 new mortar- and bazooka-proof concrete strongpoints.

Although they tied down 82,000 men (mostly non-European), after a very thorough initial search-and-destroy operation throughout the Delta they did allow the thinning of internal security troops; and coincided with a major mobilisation of the 'Vietnamese National Army' from around 65,000 to around 110,000 regulars and auxiliaries.

The Legion had for some months been providing 'on the job training' to Vietnamese battalions affiliated to Legion regiments, and since 1946 each unit had had its own hard-bitten local 'supplementary commando', often of 'turned' Viet Minh. Now each Legion regiment was ordered to change one or even two of its battalions to composite establishment (534 Europeans to 292 Vietnamese), and each battalion to form a composite (in practice, largely Vietnamese) company. There were obvious problems over language, racial prejudice, shortage of reliable cadres, the presence (as in all SE Asian armies) of the troops' families, and over what we may call differences in military culture – the Vietnamese tended to be fast but of fragile morale, the white légionnaires determined but slow. Some units were better than others; but in general, combat exerience vindicated the plan. It at least provided desperately needed manpower; by the height of the war many battalions were up to 50 per cent locally raised.

De Lattre used this opportunity to increase his reserve. The Groupes Mobiles (an idea brought from Morocco, to whose open spaces they were better suited) typically consisted of three truck-borne infantry battalions, of which only one was usually European; an artillery or heavy mortar battery; a small armoured car and/or tank element; and sometimes additional engineer or amphibious assets. With around 1,200 men and 120 vehicles, the GMs performed well in the Delta battles of early 1951; once sent into the jungle, swamps or hills they were much

M29C radio command vehicle of the tactical HQ of GA2, photographed here during operations with the 13e DBLE. (ECPA)

Tonkin, 1954: LVT-A4 amphibious fire support vehicle of the 1er REC's 2e GA, fitted with the 75mm howitzer turret from the M8 HMC. By now the 2e GA had three squadrons (one non-Legion) each with 33 'Crabs'; three squadrons each with eleven LVT-4 'Alligators' carrying Vietnamese infantry; and six LVT-A4s. (ECPA)

more vulnerable, and suffered some memorable ambushes. Legion units were often included in Groupes Mobiles; such duty was more popular than the morale-sapping life of the small outposts. Famous fights included that by II/2e REI with GM.4 near Ngoc Thap during Operation Lorraine, November 1952; and by II/13e DBLE with GM.4 near Yen Leo during Operation Mouette in October 1953 – a battle which also involved III/13e and I/5e REI.

MAJOR ACTIONS

There is only room for the briefest notes on a few of the best-known individual Legion actions of the war (the interested reader is directed to the bibliography at the end of the text for sources of fuller accounts).

Phu Tong Hoa, July 1948

The strings of posts along Routes Coloniales 3, 3bis and 4 in NE Tonkin, shadowing the Chinese frontier, were always particularly vulnerable; the road, meandering and switch-backing through forested hills and jagged limestone buttes, was an ambusher's heaven. The posts were always overlooked; the 3e REI garrisons were too small to dominate the surrounding country; and it was often as much as they could do to secure the roads on which they depended for their supply convoys. In July 1948 three officers and 101 men of 2e Cie., I/3e REI held Phu Tong Hoa on RC.3 – a post with nine-foot earth walls, a few mines, thin wire supplemented by the usual bamboo *chevaux-de-frise*, corner blockhouses, and brick interior buildings. They had two old 37mm guns, one 81mm and two 61mm mortars.

On the misty, rainy night of 25 July the post – isolated by several ambushes on the roads north and south – was attacked by two VM battalions, trained on a life-size model of the fort, and supported by 75mm and 37mm guns, mortars and machine-guns. The bombardment began at 7pm, soon breaching the west wall and smashing Blockhouse 1; Capt. Cardinal and Lt. Charlotton were mortally wounded; and command fell to S/Lt. Bevalot, just 15 days off the boat. At 9.15pm the barrage stopped, trumpets were heard, and a human wave of infantry fell on the west and north defences. The VM soon got inside the post, and for two hours isolated groups of légionnaires fought hand-to-hand from the various buildings and weapon-pits, with rifles, grenades, bayonets, knives, and vertically fired mortar bombs. At one time three of the four blockhouses had fallen. At about 11pm the rain and mist cleared, the moon gave better visibility, and the attack lost momentum; the blockhouses were recaptured, and the VM finally fell back – carrying most of

Tonkin, 1951: légionnaires of III/5e REI ride M24 Chaffee tanks of 2e Esc./1er, RCC, Groupe Blindé 2, during Operation Tulipe. The landscape, dominated by wooded limestone pinnacles, is typical of the Tonkinese 'High Region'; the success of Viet Minh ambushes is not hard to understand. (ECPA)

The Groupe d'Escadrons Amphibie of Ier REC typically comprised one Crab squadron and one Alligator squadron (numbered e.g. 3^{e} and 13^{e} Escadrons respectively). The latter had command, recovery and fire support vehicles as well as troop carriers – like 'Colmar', pictured here in February 1952 during Operation Crachin near Ninh Giang – for the four platoons of locally recuited infantry. (ECPA)

their dead, although 89 were found in the wire. Legion casualties were 23 dead, 48 wounded. It took three days and three separate attempts to get a relief column through from Cao Bang; when Lt.Col. Simon, CO of I/3^{e} REI, finally arrived on the evening of 28 July, S/Lt. Bevalot – who had 39 men left on their feet – turned out a guard of honour.

Route Coloniale 4, October 1950

Phu Tong Hoa was a deliberate exercise to test whether Giap's main force could take a European garrison in pitched battle. The answer had been 'probably – with more men and guns'; and in May 1949, with both, he took Dong Khe on RC.4, before withdrawing in the face of a parachuted relief force. In the battle for RC.4 he would have an easier target: the French came out into the jungle, and gave him a series of giant ambushes to fight instead of a positional battle.

The fall of China to the Communists in 1949 had brought Giap priceless advantages. Safe depots and training camps were set up north of the Chinese border; heavy weapons, artillery, field radios, and instructors were provided; and by October Giap had two complete divisions ready and a third nearly worked up.

By autumn 1950 the French had decided that RC.4 was untenable. The plan for Col. Charton's three battalions (including III/3^{e} REI) to withdraw south-eastwards down the road from Cao Bang, gathering other garrisons as they went, was thoroughly compromised. Giap had time to assemble in the hills his main force, Regts. 36, 88, 99, 165, 174, 175, 209, 246, and regional units – eventually, a total of 30 battalions with artillery support. A 3,500-man (mainly Moroccan) column under Col. Lepage was assembled at Lang Son to march up RC.4; but on 18 September the road was cut when Dong Khe was taken again, 5^{e} and 6^{e} Cies. of II/3^{e} REI being wiped out by five VM battalions with strong artillery. Both columns would now have to fight their way along the road to effect a junction, helped by the dropping of 1er BEP at That Khe. On

1 October Lepage started north from That Khe; on the 3rd, Charton started south from Cao Bang; and by that night both forces were blocked, dislocated, and taking significant casualties.

Heavy mist prevented air support. Both columns took to the hill tracks south-west of RC.4, abandoning vehicles and heavy equipment to attempt a rendezvous. This was achieved, against constant attacks, late on 7 October, by which time all units were so shattered that the commanders decided to disperse their men into platoon-sized parties to attempt to slip through the jungle to That Khe, where a second para battalion, 3e BCCP, was dropped on the 8th. But on 10 October, while survivors were still straggling in, its garrison abandoned That Khe, the para unit dying almost to a man in major ambushes. Giap attacked everywhere; panic gripped the French command; and by 18 October many posts and towns had been abandoned, some far from any threat. The whole of Tonkin north of the Delta fell, uniting the Viet Bac with China and opening new opportunities for Giap.

The French lost some 4,800 dead and missing (including 2½ Legion battalions wiped out) and about 2,000 wounded; Giap captured enough weapons to equip a division, including artillery, plus some 1,300 tons of supplies. The Viet Minh would from now on be taken seriously by every officer on the French staff.

Eric Morgan was 19 when he arrived in Indochina in 1951; here, back in North Africa three and a half years later, he has visibly matured. Morgan (who never came across another British légionnaire, serving mostly with Germans and Russians) saw considerable action in the course of many month-long jungle fighting patrols, and the defence of fixed positions in Tonkin: 'If you lived, you learned; if you learned, you lived...' He wears the breast badge of 6e REI, then a transit unit in Tunisia; and on his left shoulderstrap that of his former combat regiment, 2e REI. (Courtesy Eric Morgan)

Hoa Binh, November 1951-February 1952

By early 1951 the booty of RC.4, Chinese support (including modern US weapons captured in Korea), and up-grading of regional units enabled the completion of five VM divisions (304th, 308th, 312th, 316th and 320th, each with 12 battalions and integral artillery); plus seven artillery and eight engineer battalions. For once impatient, Giap threw 22,000 men of the 308th and 312th straight into conventional assaults on De Lattre's Delta defences in January 1951 at Vinh Yen. After early success

M51A tank (and hidden in smoke, a supporting M8 75mm howitzer motor carriage) during Operation Sauterelles in Annam, August 1952; note Ier REC badge on the side plate. Note, too, the intriguing use by the crew of what seem to be black peaked field caps very reminiscent of the Wehrmacht M1943. (ECPA)

Tonkin, 1953: a battalion of 3^{e} REI on parade, wearing the khaki drill summer/tropical full dress with epaulettes, sashes, citation lanyards and decorations – see also Plate E1. The weapons are MAS.36 rifles, FM.24/29 LMGs, and MAT.49 SMGs. With one magnificent exception, note the relative youth of these faces; by this time the average age of légionnaires in Indochina was in the very early twenties, exposing the myth that 'Dien Bien Phu was fought by German Waffen-SS veterans'. (ECPA)

they were driven back, with 6,000 dead and as many wounded, by De Lattre's rapidly airlifted reinforcements and air support (using napalm for the first time). In March the 316th were beaten off at Mao Khe; and in May-June the 304th, 308th and 320th were badly mauled on the Day River. Giap learned his lesson: it was too soon to attack the Delta garrison, with its internal lines, artillery and airfields. The *Chuc luc* withdrew into the hills once more.

With the Delta apparently safe and swept clean, in November 1951 De Lattre launched a major drive 40km west from the Delta to recapture Hoa Binh, an important centre on RC.6 and a loop of the Black River, abandoned the year before. Airdrops and overland columns seized the town, the routes into it, and – after difficult fighting – some of the hills dominating those routes. But the rebuilt 304th, 308th and 312th Divs. steadily tightened their grip around the corridor in weeks of see-saw fighting, involving I/2^{e}, I/5^{e} & III/5^{e} REI, II/ & III/13^{e} DBLE and both Legion para units. While often victorious tactically, the French were soon paying a heavy price for no exploitable strategic advantage; the corridor proved untenable, and the task force fought their way back to the Delta – with some difficulty – in February 1952. Viet tactics had included eerily skilful night infiltration, 'human wave' assaults apparently reckless of losses, and formidable artillery too well hidden to be countered by French aircraft – which met increasingly serious ground fire.

Phu Doan & Na San, November 1952

In 1952 Giap manoeuvred three divisions deep into the Thai Highlands, taking large stretches of countryside and many remote posts and threatening the Laotian border. The new C-in-C Gen. Salan made an attempt in late October to draw him back by cutting off his bases;

Operation Lorraine sent 30,000 men north-west from the Delta up RC.2 towards Phu Doan. This achieved some success, destroying major VM depots; but Giap kept his nerve, staying in the border hills while his forces in place brought enough pressure on the narrow, 150km corridor to force French withdrawal in mid-November in a costly running battle. It seemed that the French could hold the Delta, and – with maximum effort – could punch through to most objectives outside it; but they could not hold them.

Meanwhile, reinforcements could only be placed in the way of the VM divisions in the Thai Highlands by airlift; in November Salan reinforced and fortified the airfield at Na San to act as a regional bastion, and the III/3^{e} and III/5^{e} REI were among ten battalions flown in. For once Giap's intelligence reports let him down; thinking the garrison much weaker, he sent four regiments into repeated attacks on 23 November-2 December, and was driven off badly mauled. This victory, due to unusual circumstances, bred among the French staff a dangerous optimism about the potential of isolated 'airheads' far from the Delta.

Dien Bien Phu, November 1953-May 1954

In November 1953 the French planned to frustrate a renewed VM move towards Laos by planting a major 'airhead' at Dien Bien Phu, a valley-bottom airstrip in the Thai Highlands some 270km from the Delta bases. Seized without difficulty by paratroopers, it was fortified and heavily garrisoned by air during the following weeks, supposedly as a base for offensive operations – or as an anvil against which the hammer of artillery and air power would smash the attacking VM – but the strategic priorities seem to have been muddled. Ten battalions were flown in to join the paras: I/2^{e} REI, III/3^{e} REI, I/ & III/13^{e} DBLE; four North African; and two local. The camp had 28 heavy guns, ten M24 tanks, and six Bearcats on the airstrip. But with 10,000 men to supply, the French airlift capability was inadequate to fly in the engineer stores to construct serious shell-proof defences – and in any case, the French staff did not believe that Giap could move his artillery hundreds of miles across appalling terrain from the Viet Bac bases. For the last time, they underestimated his ingenuity and ruthlessness.

Massive conscription of civilian labour and an epic of logistic improvisation enabled Giap to assemble and conceal in the surrounding hills, by early March 1954, some 200 guns of 75mm and up, scores of heavy mortars and RCLs, a 64-gun Chinese-manned 37mm AA regiment – and nearly 50,000 men of the 304th, 308th, 312th and 316th Divisions. Strong French sorties in December were turned back with serious loss; soon patrols in the valley itself ran into daily skirmishes; and on 31 December a desultory shelling began. The story of the siege has been told at length elsewhere; the essentials are as follows.

On the afternoon of 13 March a massive artillery bombardment struck the flimsy bunkers and open gun-pits. That night the III/13^{e} DBLE was shelled to pieces and overrun by waves of infantry on the important outlying north-eastern defensive position codenamed Beatrice. On the night of the 15th the northern strongpoint Gabrielle also fell. In the fortnight that followed the whole camp continued to take heavy punishment; the enemy began to seep inwards all round the pattern of strongpoints (the valley was too big for a continuous

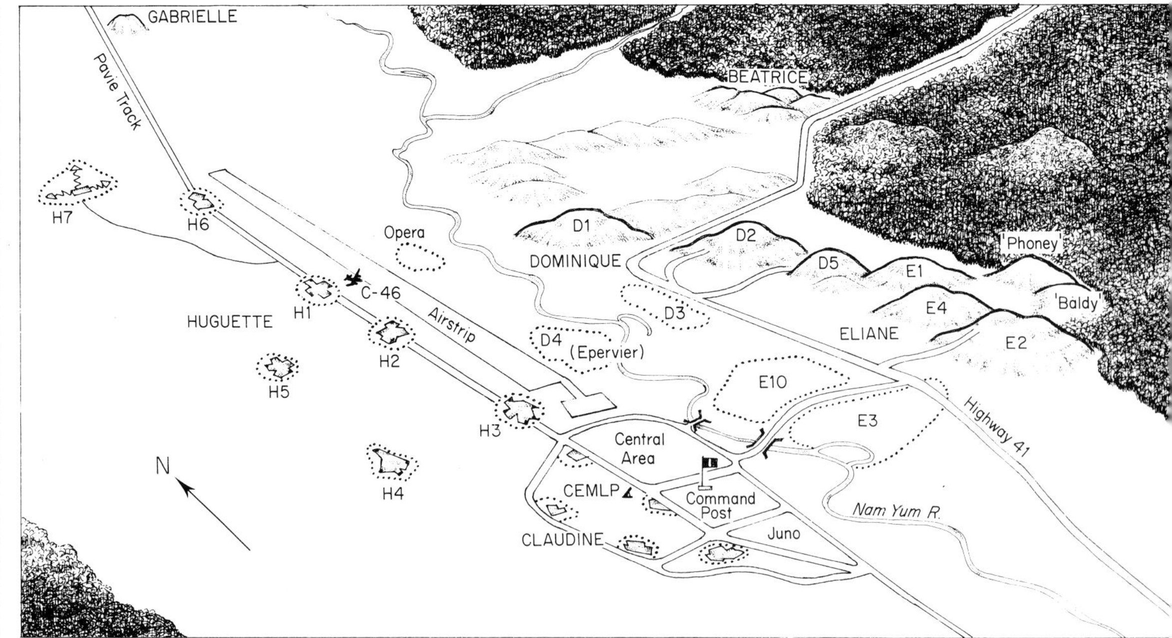

Simplified map of Dien Bien Phu, Spring 1954. The loss of strongpoints Beatrice (III/13e DBLE) and Gabrielle on 13-15 March allowed Giap to bring his artillery and anti-aircraft guns much closer to the airstrip and central camp. Dominique 1 fell on 31 March; 'Phoney' and 'Baldy' were in Viet hands throughout, the latter connected to the vital Eliane 2 by a saddle allowing direct infantry assaults. Initially I/2e REI held the Huguette strongpoints – increasingly hard to hold against pressure down the airstrip from the north; and I/13e DBLE the Claudines – which held out to the end; but during April-May men of both units were moved around at need. III/3e were isolated 4km south at Isabelle (not shown here).

perimeter); the Bearcats, hopelessly vulnerable, had to fly out; the enemy AA guns were installed ever closer to the camp; and the last Dakota to brave the fire took off on the 27th. From now on all reinforcements and supplies had to be parachuted, in the face of intense flak. The monsoon rains broke on the 29th, further hampering the air force. From the end of March III/3^{e} REI were completely cut off in Isabelle, the southernmost strongpoint which was 4km from the main position.

From 30 March to 6 April savage attacks fell on the para units holding the 'five hills' – the eastern positions codenamed Eliane and Dominique; and on Huguette, the north-west quadrant of the main position, held by I/2^{e} REI. The I/13^{e} DBLE held Claudine, in the south-west; but as the weeks of fighting dragged on, and positions fell one by one – sometimes to be retaken in desperate counter-attacks, sometimes not – the survivors of the various units were moved around at need, eventually fighting in mixed *ad hoc* battle-groups. Both I/2^{e} and I/13^{e} would at various dates supply companies to fight on Eliane 2, and men of I/13^{e} would fight in the Huguettes.

The fighting resembled that on the Western Front of 1917: chronically short of every necessity, the defenders clung to muddy trenches dissolving under rain and shellfire, while the enemy dug ever closer, cutting off isolated strongpoints before pouring over the wire at night in sacrificial assaults. The rapidly dwindling artillery, and the aircraft which managed the long flight through the monsoon from the Delta bases, were quite unable to silence the VM guns or seriously interdict the besiegers' supply lines. Giap's regiments suffered dreadful casualties (by the end, perhaps 8,000 dead and twice that number wounded, in an army with virtually no medical service); but in the end, in the first week of May, the camp was simply smothered by a last series of assaults. Resistance ended in the main camp on 7 May; an attempted break-out that night by III/3^{e} REI from Isabelle failed.

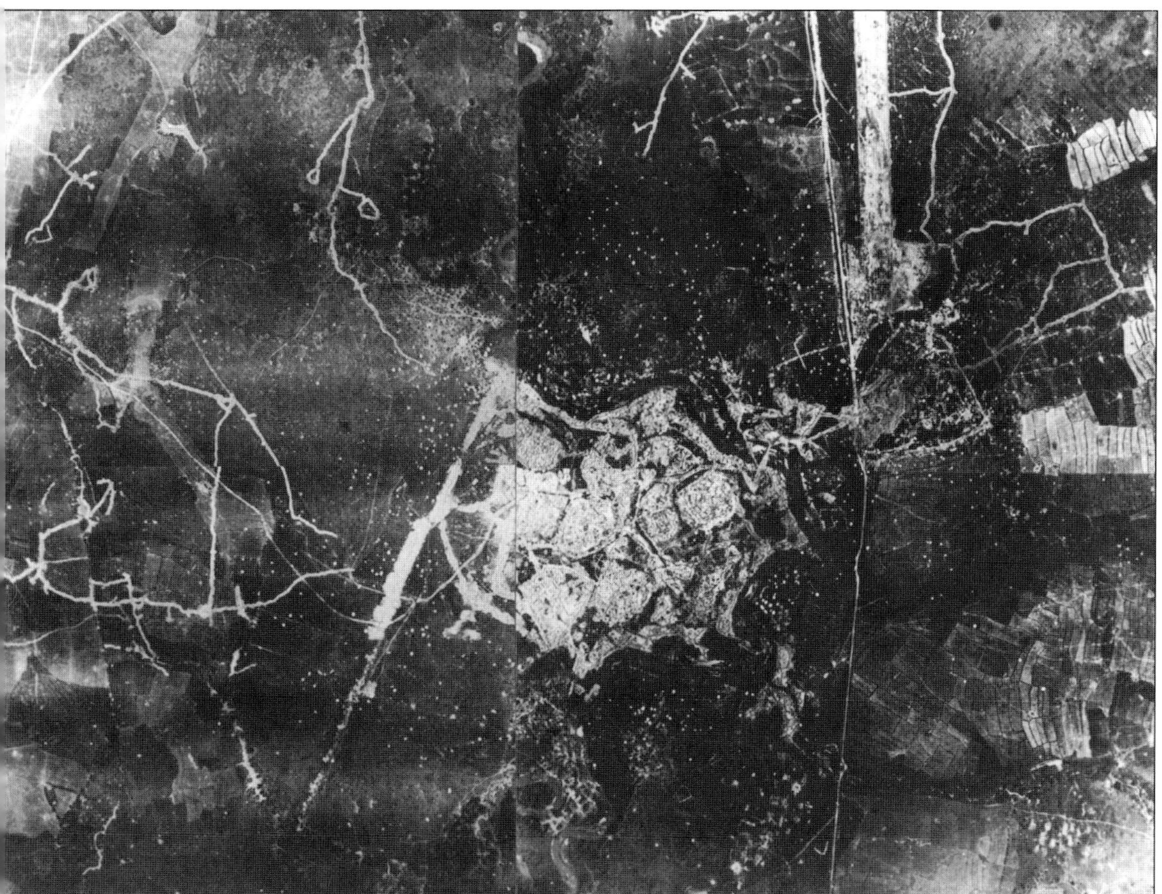

Dien Bien Phu, April 1954: composite aerial photograph of strongpoint Isabelle, isolated 4km south of the main camp, which was held by III/3e REI. Note the auxiliary airstrip and Highway 41 at north-west (top right); the light earth spoil showing the main areas of trenching and dug-outs; the light spots over all, indicating both shell and mortar holes and discarded parachute canopies from supply drops; and the approach trenches of Giap's 304th Division advancing like root tendrils. (ECPA)

Dien Bien Phu cost the CEFEO some 2,200 dead, 1,700 missing presumed dead, and 6,450 wounded. Of these, at least 1,500 of the dead and missing and perhaps 4,000 wounded were légionnaires; it is impossible to be exact, since only some 3,000 of the 6,000-7,000 men marched into captivity by the Viets ever returned. The I/2e REI, III/3e REI, I/ & III/13e DBLE, both Legion para battalions, and three Legion mortar companies were wiped out, together with many volunteers from the 3e and 5e REI who had parachuted in during the siege.

Renewed attacks on the Delta followed; but within weeks France had agreed to a general ceasefire in Indochina, and the subsequent Geneva talks would lead to the partitioning of Vietnam into two states, a Communist north and an independent south.

REGIMENTAL SERVICE IN INDOCHINA

The following notes are the most superficial record, but give an idea of the wide-ranging part played by Legion battalions.

2e REI

Retitled from RMLE/EO Jan.1945; landed Feb.1946. Pacification of south Annam. I/2e to Tonkin, Dec.1946; ops. in Tonkin until 1954 – Hoa Binh, RC.6 battles, Nov.1951-Feb.1952; wiped out at Dien Bien Phu, spring 1954. II/2e to Tonkin 1951; ops. with Groupe Mobile 4 in Delta; to Laos, 1953-54 – Plain of Jars, Luang Prabang. III/2e to Tonkin, May

1951; in central Annam, 1952-54. IV/2^{e} raised late 1949, Vietnamese troops with Legion cadre; central Annam 1950-54.

3^{e} REI

Landed April (I & II/3^{e}) and June (III/3^{e}) 1946; pacification of Cochinchina; Mekong Delta. I/3^{e} to Tonkin, March 1947; II & III/3^{e} follow, Oct.1947. Ops. along RC.4; 2^{e} Cie. hold Phu Tong Hoa, July 1948; 5^{e} & 6^{e} Cies. lost at Dong Khe, Sept.1950; III/3^{e} wiped out on RC.4, Oct.1950. Reorganised Hanoi; III/3^{e}, re-formed from Bn. de Marche 1er REI, at Na San, Nov.1952-Apr.1953; 1951, Vietnamese IV & V/3^{e} raised. Almost continuous ops. in Tonkin, 1951-54; II/3^{e} to Laos, April 1953; with Groupe Mobile 6, Dec.1953. III/3^{e} wiped out again at Dien Bien Phu, spring 1954.

5^{e} REI

Bn. de Marche returned from China, Feb.1946; to Saigon, Sept.; disbanded Nov.1946. I/5^{e} re-formed from III/6^{e}, Nov.1949; ops. on RC.6, Feb.-March 1950; ops. around Hanoi, April-May; Tourane, Hue, summer 1950. II/5e re-formed from V/4e, Nov.1949; ops. Tonkin, Tourane, Hue, summer 1950; supporting role during RC.4 battles, Oct.1950. III/5e raised March 1950. All bns. on RC.18, Mon Cai area, late 1950. Building De Lattre Line, 1951; Vietnamese IV/5e raised spring 1951, III/5e with Groupement Blindé 2. Nov.1951-Feb.1952; I/5e & III/5e in Hoa Binh/ RC.6 battles; all bns., continuous ops. Tonkin, 1952-53. III/5e at Na San, Nov.1952-April 1953, in central Annam summer 1953; II/5e covers return of paras from Lang Son drop, July 1953; I/5e in southern Delta Oct.-Nov.1953, to Laos early 1954; II & III/5e ops. in Delta. 5e REI in Hanoi after Dien Bien Phu; to Annam, Nov.1954; to Saigon, Sept.1955; II/5e last Legion unit to leave Vietnam, 12 March 1956.

Algeria, mid-1950s: a lieutenant of Legion infantry – probably 3e REI, in the Aurès – with an ALN suspect. The officer's white or very pale KD *képi*-cover has holes cut at the front to display his gold grenade badge and a section of his rank braid – a practice dating back to the 1920s. Armed with an M1 carbine, he wears M1947 green fatigues with a camouflage-veil scarf, and a French copy of the US web pistol belt with US carbine clip pouches. (Courtesy Wayne Braby)

13^{e} DBLE

Landed March 1946; ops. Cochinchina, southern Annam; Plaine des Joncs, Mekong Delta. 1948, II/13^{e} to Cambodia, then central Annam; III/13^{e} round Hoc Mon, near Saigon. 1949, central Annam; Vietnamese IV/13^{e} raised. 1950, all bns. Hoc Mon. 1951, II & III/13^{e} to Tonkin; building De Lattre Line, and ops. Delta; Nov.1951-Feb.1952, Hoa Binh/RC.6 battles. 1952, III/13^{e} to central Annam. Oct.1953, II/13^{e} with Groupe Mobile 4, northern Annam/southern Tonkin. I & III/13^{e} wiped out at Dien Bien Phu, spring 1954.

1er REC

Landed Saigon Jan.1947 without vehicles; ops.as infantry, Tourane, Hue. Received British Coventry armoured & Humber scout cars, Bren carriers (4^{e} & 5^{e} Esc. April 1947, 3^{e} & 6^{e} Esc. June-July); 1er & 2^{e}, armed trucks and jeeps, 5^{e} & 6^{e} Esc. receive 30 armoured jeeps, 1er Esc. five H.39 tanks later in 1947. End 1947, 1er & 2^{e} Esc in Cochinchina, 3^{e} at Tourane, 4^{e} Hue, 5^{e} Dong Hoi, 6^{e} Phan Tri; road and convoy security.

Three classic weapons of the indochina War: the MAT.49 sub-machine-gun, the old FM24/29 light machine-gun, and the M24 Chafee tank. Coincidentally this photo also points up the difference in outline between the US M1 helmet (left) and the French M1951. (ECPA)

Early 1948, *1ère Groupe d'Escadrons* (HQ, 1er & 2e Esc.) in Cochinchina receive US M29 Weasel armed light amphibious vehicles; successful ops. in wetlands 1948-49; 6e Esc. joins early 1950. 2e GE (3e, 4e & 5e Esc.) at Hue, Quang Tri & Dong Hoi, central Annam in 1950, with US M8 & M20 armoured cars, half-tracks. From late 1950, 1er GE squadrons each receive platoon US LVT4 Alligator armoured amphibious personnel carriers; Vietnamese infantry element added. 1er GE, at Tourane, becomes *1er Groupement Autonome* (Independent Group), summer 1951; 2e GA formed Haiphong, Tonkin with similar equipment; 7e Esc. at Hue. Steady increase in strength, equipment, 1951-54; continuous operations all over wetlands, rivers, and inshore coastal areas of Vietnam. By mid-1953 the *Groupements d'Escadrons Amphibies* and other 1er REC regimental assets total 14 combat and four support squadrons, fielding mainly M29s, LVT4s, LVT(A)4s, half-tracks, M8 armoured cars and 75mm HMC howitzers, and M5A1 Stuart light tanks, performing wide range of security, support, and assault operations all over Vietnam.

Specialist units

One of many shortages hampering the CEFEO was that of specialist personnel for the mechanised units and support services. The Legion channelled recruits with useful skills into the REC, or a number of technical units formed locally (which would represent nearly 20 per cent of total Legion strength in-country). Examples were the truck drivers of 40e Cie. de Camions Bennes; the vehicle mechanics and fitters of 2e Cie.(Moyenne) de Réparation; and the sappers of the 21e Cie., 61e Bataillon de Génie.

One famous local innovation was the *Rafale*, an improvised armoured train operated by the 2e REI in the area Ninh Hoa, Phat Thiet and Nha Trang in southern Annam. Built in winter 1948-49, it had two locomotives and 14 wagons, including a command and radio wagon, an ambulance wagon, a cookhouse wagon, and two wagons loaded with rails and sleepers pushed ahead of the forward locomotive to explode mines. Armament included a 40mm Bofors gun, a 20mm cannon with infra-red sights, eight twin Reibel machine guns, an 81mm mortar fixed to an old Japanese artillery mounting, and a 60mm mortar. The crew numbered about 100 légionnaires and local auxiliaries. The veteran of many ambushes and firefights, the train was never destroyed, and survived to be abandoned at the end of the war.

In all, 314 officers, 1,071 NCOs and 8,997 men of the Foreign Legion were killed or died of wounds in Indochina, 1946-54; some 1,100 were listed as missing.

MOROCCO 1945-57

The French Protectorate over Morocco, which dated from before the First World War, was to last until March 1956, and the last French garrisons until 1957. The traditional 'Regiment of Morocco' had been the old 4^{e} REI; and in April/May 1946 the 4^{e} DBLE – a briefly active Second World War garrison unit – was re-formed with battalions at Fez and Meknes and a motorised company at Ksar-es-Souk; it would eventually rise to a strength of four battalions. A group of motorised companies based on Agadir since 1944, attached administratively to

Haiphong, 1954: Sherman ARVs of the Ier REC parade during the visit of a French government minister. (ECPA)

the 3e REI, was now retitled *Groupement Porté Légion Étrangère du Maroc* (GPLEM).

In June 1947 the IV/4e DBLE was shipped to Madagascar. There it would serve a dual security and public works role, at first as the Bn. de M.4e DBLE and later, from May 1949 until its dispersal in December 1951, under the *Groupe des Unités de la Légion Étrangère à Madagascar*, its sister units being an engineer company and the armoured jeeps of 4e Esc./2e REC.

In October 1947 each of the other three battalions gave up one company for the new 2e Bataillon Étranger de Parachutistes, and the old title 4e REI was revived. In 1949 the III/4e was shipped to Tonkin to help re-form the 5e REI, and other drafts followed. By 1951 only one battalion remained, at Meknes; that December the IV/4e returned from Madagascar to Fez. The first signs of the anti-French disorder which would lead to Moroccan independence came in April 1952. Apart from the 4^{e}, elements of the 1er REI and the whole 2^{e} REI became involved in 'police' operations. So did the 2^{e} REC, a brief pre-war creation which had been re-formed in 1946 to feed men out to the 1er REC in Indochina; it absorbed the latter's 2^{e} Groupe Amphibie when it returned from the Far East in October 1955.

Towards the end of this period a new type of unit emerged. In the winter of 1956-57 the I & II/4e REI and the GPLEM were amalgamated into a new motorised 4e REI, of two separate Groupes each with an HQ element and three truck-borne Compagnies Portées, with an integral armoured car platoon equipped with American M8s. This would come to be a model for other motorised infantry 'intervention' units during the fighting in Algeria. The 4e REI's last company drove over the border into Algeria on 18 April 1957, ending 50 years of Legion history in Morocco.

ALGERIA 1954-62

After a brutal local rising, bloodily avenged, at Sétif in May 1945, Algeria had remained ostensibly quiet until 1954; but a number of Arab and Berber underground nationalist groups had been forming, and groping their way towards unity of purpose. Defeat in Indochina robbed the French of much of their *baraka* – spiritual force – in Muslim eyes; and on 1 November 1954 the National Liberation Front (FLN) issued a general call to arms, attacking small military and police targets in many areas to obtain weapons. Success was patchy; during winter 1954-55, while French troops slogged through the cold, rainy hills of the Aurès and Kabylie highlands, it was enough of an achievement for most of the few hundred guerrillas simply to survive in scattered bands.

The ALN (National Liberation Army) faced far greater difficulties than had the Viet Minh. It was not truly unified; it was weakly armed; and the civilian population was far less automatically supportive. Most Muslims were traditionalists, long accustomed to French rule, and apathetic if not downright hostile towards the insurgents. A white settler population of over a million was much longer established and better integrated than in Indochina; while the extreme demands of these 'Pieds Noirs' were politically destabilising to weak, short-lived French governments, they did provide keen eyes and ears, and a pool of high-quality recruits.

The regiments returning from the Far East in winter 1954-55 were posted to various regions with local responsibility for hunting down ALN bands; the 3e REI, the first Legion unit to return, were sent into the wilderness of the Aurès mountains to relieve a 1er REI task force. French success, too, was patchy; the bare hills were not as dangerous as the jungle gorges of Tonkin, but offered plentiful hiding places, and French units were largely roadbound.

Spring 1955 brought an increased tempo of incidents; there were isolated ambushes of French convoys and patrols, as well as a growing campaign of selective atrocities – often of medieval cruelty – against both anti-ALN Muslims such as village elders, and white settlers who had friendly relations with Muslims. Hundreds of white-owned farms – the country's economic base – were destroyed. The governor-general introduced an imaginative and well-funded 'hearts and minds' programme; the ALN countered it in the classic fashion.

In August 1955 an appalling massacre of white civilians around Philippeville was followed by predictably savage reprisals, giving the spiral of mutual hatred another twist and silencing moderate voices on both sides. New, effective ALN leaders emerged from the first year's fighting; guerrilla strength increased to perhaps 15,000, and their intimidating grip on the rural population tightened. During 1955 the 13^e^ DBLE returned to Algeria, taking over a sector in the far north-east on the Tunisian border.

In 1956 the number of clashes increased steadily, as did the size of some of the bands encountered. The first major defections from French Algerian units were recorded, drawing suspicion on the rest. The vengeful ruthlessness of both guerrillas and soldiers became more marked, increasing the misery of the Muslim population. Under pressure from the 'Pieds Noirs' France announced a massive increase in the garrison – from around 200,000 to 500,000 – including conscripts and reservists.

Simplified map of northern Algeria – the southern CSPL bases are not shown.

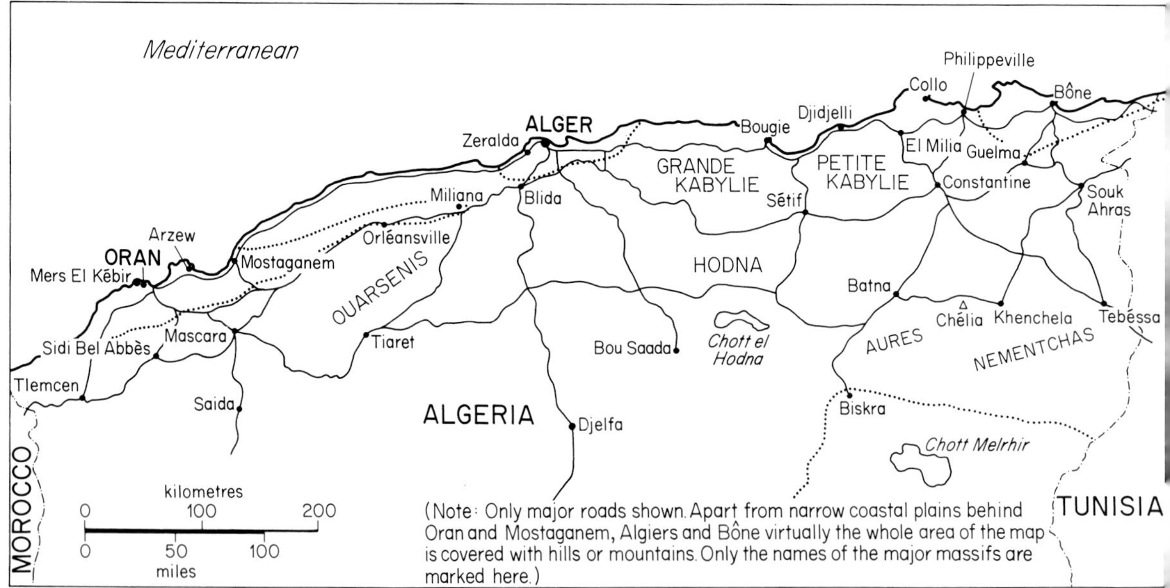

Aurès Mountains, 1954-55: at this date 3e REI was the only Legion unit to have returned from Indochina. This photo has been identified elsewhere as showing Cpl. Dembowski of IV/3e comforting Cpl. Boenke – shot in the chest during a contact in thick cover – while awaiting casevac. (Courtesy Wayne Braby)

March brought negotiated independence to neighbouring Morocco and Tunisia, although French bases would remain for some time. This would give the ALN the safe external refuges essential to successful guerrilla movements; but with no comparison with the help China had given the Viet Minh. Tunisia was too weak to provoke a French re-occupation, and gave sanctuary only; Morocco was ruled by a subtle monarch hostile to the FLN's politics. The ALN would build up its forces and depots in these external camps; but as bases for attacks into Algeria they would fail. During 1956 the 2e REI returned from Morocco to north-east Algeria, and the 5e REI from Indochina, deploying in the north-west, to join the guard on the Tunisian and Moroccan frontiers respectively.

The Anglo-French débâcle at Suez in November 1956 damaged French prestige and morale, and at last brought the ALN much needed supplies of weapons from President Nasser of Egypt (before late 1956 it was said that they had only ten machine guns and 20 mortars in the whole country). The French had also grown stronger, however. The flow of conscripts provided manpower for the static network of 'sector' troops, and would increasingly free the paratroop and Legion units for more aggressive operations; and a steadily growing fleet of troop-carrying helicopters would provide the means of fast and flexible insertion. Once the Suez sideshow was over, paratroop officers with long experience of guerrilla warfare in Indochina would concentrate on developing effective tactics based on quick reaction to sightings and relentless pursuit on the ground. The year 1957 would mark a turning-point.

Algeria, c.1959: Legion infantry on patrol in the endless scrub, where they could tread on an enemy before seeing him. Note bulging M1951 rucksacks with rolled tent-quarters and khaki wool greatcoats stowed on top. The man at left carries the AA.52 LMG, which began to replace the FM.24/29 by 1957; the antenna of an American SCR.300 radio can be seen at right. (Courtesy Wayne Braby)

Only paratroop units were involved in the notorious 'Battle of Algiers' in January-April and June-October 1957, which not only stopped the ALN's urban bombing campaign but virtually wiped out the organisation in the capital, causing a crisis of morale countrywide. The French 'hearts and minds' programme was bearing fruit; the stick to accompany this carrot was the forced resettlement of huge numbers of wretched civilians, creating free-fire zones and denying ALN bands their only source of rations. The rugged hinterland did not have much overhead cover, and when guerrillas were forced to move they were vulnerable to air interdiction – which the French air force, far stronger than in Vietnam, brought to a fine art. ALN losses – and even defections –

In winter 1955-56 the HQ of I/13e DBLE was at this school – burnt out by the ALN – at El Ouldja in eastern Constantine Province. The transport park of GMC 'deuce-and-a-half' trucks should not give the wrong impression: although trucked to their areas of operations, the légionnaires could only penetrate the hill country on their feet. They slogged up and down 'the *djebel* and the *bled*' for weeks at a time, sleeping in pup-tents in extremes of heat and cold, and living on very basic combat rations. (Courtesy Wayne Braby)

mounted appreciably. At Agounennda outside Algiers in May Col. Bigeard's 3^{e} RPC fixed and smashed probably the best ALN unit in Algeria – 300 men of Wilaya 4 led by Si Azedine. Heartened by clear-cut victories, the army could turn with confidence in autumn 1957 to the task of closing the frontiers across which the ALN must bring men and weapons if they were ever to build up their forces in-country.

The battle of the frontiers, 1957-58

September 1957 saw the completion of the 'Morice Line', a system of defence in depth which stretched along 200 miles of the Tunisian border; defences were also being erected on the Moroccan frontier, but the Tunisian camps – where 10,000 ALN waited to join the increasingly desperate bands inside Algeria – were always the greatest threat. Extensively wired, electrified, mined, electronically monitored, and patrolled night and day by mechanised units and aircraft, this line – like all passive defences – could be breached; but not without drawing the attention of its guardians.

In winter 1957-58 the ALN tried every means and tactic to cut their way through the 'barrages' and to force-march away from the breaches, dispersing into thick cover before the paras, the armour, the artillery and the fighter-bombers could locate them. They tried crossing in small single parties; in multiple groups, some diversionary; in companies; and finally in 300-strong battalions, hoping to fight their way out of trouble if intercepted during the vital 24 hours when they were still close to the

The American M8 armoured car equipped the 1er REC until April 1957 – the 'Royal Foreigners' are presumably pictured here, since Rachaya was the 1er REC's most famous battle-honour. The crews wear a one-piece coverall version of the M1947 green fatigue uniform, which it closely resembled. (Courtesy Wayne Braby)

frontier. Nothing worked; the 80,000 French troops – including 3e and 4e REI, 13e DBLE and both RECs – learned to counter every move. In almost daily and nightly clashes the ALN suffered ever heavier casualties; the climax, a week-long battle near Soukh-Ahras in late April 1958, saw 620 of the 820 men who crossed killed or captured, along with 460 weapons. Total losses on both frontiers, October 1957-April 1958, are reckoned at 6,000 men and 4,300 weapons. The failure of the attempt to reinforce them coincided with a period of vicious internecine feuds and purges inside the ALN regional commands, skilfully exploited by French intelligence agents.

The Challe Plan, 1959-60

Gen. De Gaulle was summoned to power in France at a time of political collapse in May 1958. He appointed Gen. Challe C-in-C that December. Challe built upon success. The essence of his method was to concentrate all reserves on one sector at a time, before sending in special 'hunting commandos' of loyal Muslim *harki* auxiliaries to locate the enemy and report, while staying on their tracks. (In 1959 there were some 30,000 *harkis* in service – about twice the ALN's active strength inside Algeria.) Assembling the intervention regiments, helicopters, and tactical aircraft

The Panhard EBR F11 – a 13-ton, eight-wheeled armoured car with a 90mm cannon and three MGs – replaced the old M8 in the 1er REC from spring 1957. This was the regiment's mount during the 'battle of the frontiers', 1957-58; during one year the REC recorded 260 nights on operations along the Morice Line. The NCO at right wears a *djellaba*, and the crewman on the glacis a khaki drill beret – see Plate E3. (ECPA)

***'La maison-mère'* – Sidi-bel-Abbes, March 1960. A company of the 1er RE swings out the gates of the historic Quartier Vienot for field training or one of the Legion's regular local route marches, wearing M1946 *képis*, *chèches*, M1947 fatigues, M1946 brown leather equipment and M1951 web gaiters, with slung M1951 steel helmets and shouldered MAS.36s and FM.24/29s. (Courtesy Wayne Braby)**

to block, fix, and destroy the *katiba*, Challe's field commanders would keep the paras and légionnaires in the area, chasing down every contact, for however long it took – up to two months – to completely disperse any survivors in numbers so weak that local sector troops could then mop up.

Then the 'Challe Steamroller' would move on to another sector, and repeat the process; in the Ouarsénis in April (Operation Courroie), the Hodna and Kabylia in July (Operations Étincelles and Jumelles), northern Constantine in September (Operation Pierres Précieuses). Thousands of insurgents were killed and weapons captured, the ALN chain of command was disrupted, and previous 'no go' areas were pacified. Challe's successor then took the steamroller into the Aurès in autumn 1960 and winter 1960-61 (Operation Trident).

From this point on the military situation steadily improved. While terrorism could never be completely stamped out, the French never lost the strategic initiative. The ALN, unable to build up large conventional units inside Algeria, were increasingly forced to disperse to evade the hunters. Though well-armed with (mostly) World War II vintage small arms and machine guns, with a few bazookas and mortars, they were always – eventually – outgunned and outnumbered by the rapidly assembled intervention regiments of truck- and heli-borne paras and légionnaires, whose unit commanders became experts at weaving a noose around enemy bands by means of ground trackers, air recon-

The Hodna Mountains, north-east of the Aurès, present a positively lunar landscape. Although this area was too empty to support ALN units, they did sometimes travel through it, and légionnaires were obliged to follow. In July 1959, during Operation Etincelles, the 3e and 5e REI and half the 2e REC fought here for a week, severing all communication between the ALN's Wilaya 3 (the Kabylia regional command) and Wilaya 4 (Aurès-Nementchas), and so weakening the latter that its leaders secretly sued for peace. (Courtesy Jim Worden)

Sidi-bel-Abbes, Camerone 1960: Légionnaire Jim Worden, 1er RE – during World War II an RAF bomber pilot, and at the time of writing the long-serving Secretary of the Foreign Legion Association of Great Britain – poses for a snap in the full finery of M1946 battledress (*tenue de drap*) with *ceinture* and *epaulettes de tradition* – see Plate E1. (Courtesy Jim Worden)

naissance, helicopter insertion of radio-scouts on high ground, and fast redeployment of sub-units by helicopter.

It was work, which kept the troops out in harsh terrain for weeks on end, under canvas in extremes of heat and cold; it involved ugly encounter skirmishes in thick cover; and even if French casualties were a tenth of the ALN's losses, they mounted up over the weeks and months. No casualty rate is 'negligible' if it involves half a squad of your best mates; to the individual infantryman, this was a hard, bitter war.

It ended in bitterness indeed. De Gaulle, accepting the inevitable, worked quietly for a negotiated peace; he had every hope that their military defeat would induce the FLN to agree terms which could salvage something for France and the settler community. But the settlers, and some soldiers, smelled only betrayal; and in April 1961 four retired generals, backed by three para regiments including the Legion's crack 1er REP, led a coup in Algiers. The *putsch* collapsed in days; the FLN were handed a priceless negotiating chip; and after a last sullen year of almost fruitless operations which kept the intervention regiments far out in the *djebels* the ceasefire came in March 1962. After 130 years, and a victorious war, the Legion was about to lose its homeland – and perhaps, even more.

Regimental Service in French North Africa

Again, these brief notes can offer only the sketchiest idea of the scope of the Legion's central role throughout the war.

1er REI/1er RE

Temporary combat units found at Sidi-bel-Abbès at various times. Aug.1954, 1er & 2e Bns. de Marche to Morocco; Sept.1954, 3e Bn. de M.

to Tunisia; Nov.1954, DB de M. to Aurès mountains, followed Jan.1955 by Bn.de M., these retitled III & IV/3e REI July 1955. Nov.1954-Jan.1955, Groupement Porté de la Légion Étrangère d'Algérie (GPLE d'Algérie) created Ain-Sefra from IV/1er REI, comprising 21e to 24e Compagnies Portées. Training units committed to local security ops., 1957-62. Total losses 53 dead, 97 wounded.

The *képi,* with a sand-khaki cover, is worn in many photos of the Legion on operations in Algeria before 1960, as by this section LMG gunner carrying an AA.52. (Courtesy Wayne Braby)

2e REI

Two battalions landed Feb.1955 Bizerta, Tunisia; June, to southern Tunisia. III/2e reformed from I/6e REI, July 1955. I/2^{e} to Morocco Sept.1955, II & III/2^{e} followed by Jan.1956; ops. in Rif mountains from HQ at Taza. Returned Algeria June 1956, to Bone and Djidjelli. Late 1956, I & III/2e disbanded; II/2e nucleus for new 'intervention' regt. 1st Group of Motorised Companies (GCP.1) with HQ and 1er, 2e & 3e Cies., first ops.Oct.1956. 1956, GPLE d'Algérie (see under 1er REI) became GCP.2 (4e-6e Cies.), joining GCP.1 at Ain-Sefra March 1957. Five years continuous mobile ops., mostly on Moroccan border; 266 dead, about 600 wounded.

3e REI

Two battalions landed Algiers Dec.1954, deployed to the Aurès. July 1955, absorbed two Bns. de M. of 1er REI as III & IV/3e; reduced to three battalions June 1956, to two Sept.1957. Ops. around Djidjelli, Taher, El Milia. Jan.1958 to Tunisian frontier 'Morice Line'; ops. around Bône, Soukh-Ahras. Oct.1958, became intervention regiment: two tactical HQs plus four companies each. Feb.1959, began ops. under 'Challe Plan' in various sectors: Ops. Étincelles, Jumelles, Pierres

Near Philippeville, 1961: légionnaires slog up yet another ridge in the pine-clad hills of north-east Algeria. (Courtesy Jim Worden)

The ceremonial uniform of the CSPLs included a doubled *burnous* cloak in midnight blue over white, a white tunic, very loose *seroual* trousers and nail sandals, together with the usual *képi,* epaulettes and blue sash. The 1ère CSPL wore short tunic sleeves and white *serouals*; the 2e, long sleeves and black *serouals* pre-1957, short sleeves thereafter; the 3e, long sleeves and black *serouals* pre-1956, white serouals thereafter; the 4e, short sleeves and white *serouals*. The escort NCOs in the 1ere and 3e CSPL *fanion* guards (here, the 3e, post-1956) carried M1822 sabres. The nearside *caporal-chef* is Vietnamese; a photo of the 2e CSPL parading shows a whole squad of Vietnamese, wearing white berets instead of *képis*. (Courtesy A.Reynolds)

Précieuses, Dordogne. July 1961, to retained French port and base at Bizerta, Tunisia, during Tunisian blockade; to Orléansville, Aug.1961; in the Ouarsénis at March 1962 ceasefire. Total casualties 197 dead, 390 wounded.

4e REI

Deployed in two GCPs to SE Algeria after crossing from Morocco, Spring 1957. 1957-58, ops. around Tebessa, Biskra, in Aurés and Nementcha mountains. June 1959, to Guelma covering Morice Line; ops. along Tunisian frontier until March 1962, at ceasefire near Négrine; 73 dead since crossing from Morocco.

5e REI

Three battalions landed Mers-el-Kebir, Feb.-April 1956; to Orléansville. Marnia-Nedroma, then Tlemcen region, Spring 1956; ops. all over NW Algeria, ending Djelfa sector summer 1958; Aug.1957, III/5e disbanded. Oct.1958, became intervention regiment: two tac HQs plus three companies each. Nov.1958, began mobile ops. around Mascara, Saida, Tiaret, Aflou, Géryville, Djelfa, helicopter ops. in Ouarsénis. July 1959, Op. Jumelles, Kabylia; Nov.1959, Collo Peninsula; Oct.1960, the Aurès, Beni-Melloul forest, Constantine, Bou-Hamama, Kenchela; Géryville,

Rear view of CSPL *légionnaires* on operations wearing the khaki drill *gandourah* desert smock, and M1950 *type TAP* webbing with MAT.49 magazine pouches. There were some brisk encounters with ALN gun-runners in the 'sand seas' of the true Sahara, notably by the 4e CSPL in the Timimoun area in Nov.-Dec.1957; one 30-man platoon marched 120km on foot in four days, over 'untruckable' sand. (Courtesy Wayne Braby)

1: Maréchal-des-logis, 1er Régiment Étranger de Cavalerie; Austria, Spring 1945
2: Adjudant, Régiment de Marche de la Légion Étrangère/Extreme Orient; Oran, 10 February 1946
3: Sergent, 2e Régiment Étranger d'Infanterie; post garrison, Annam, c.1950

A

1: Légionnaire, 13e Demi-Brigade de la Légion Étrangère; Cochinchina, 1948-50
2: Legion infantryman; Tonkin, 1950-54
3: Section light machine-gunner, Legion Infantry; Tonkin, 1950-54

B

1: Lieutenant-Colonel Charton; RC.4, October 1950

2: Légionnaire, 2e Compagnie, I/3e Régiment Étranger d'Infanterie; Phu Tong Hoa, 27 July 1948

3: Sergent, II/2e Régiment Étranger d'Infanterie, Laos, April 1954

4: Légionnaire, 1ère classe, 13e Demi-Brigade de la Légion Étrangère; Dien Bien Phu, Winter 1953-54

1: Légionnaire, Compagnie d'Instruction, 1er Régiment Étranger; Mascara, Algeria, Summer 1957
2: Sergent, 1ère Compagnie Portée, 2e Régiment Étranger d'Infanterie; Djebel Beni-Smir, Algeria, December 1960
3: Légionnaire, 1ère Compagnie Saharienne Portée de la Légion; Laghouat area, southern Algeria, c.1960

D

1: Caporal, 3e Régiment Étranger d'Infanterie; Winter guard dress, Algeria, c.1959

2: Légionnaire 1ère classe, 5e Régiment Étranger d'Infanterie; Summer walking-out dress, Algeria, c.1959

3: Sous-officier, 2e Régiment Étranger de Cavalerie; Algeria, 1959

4: Légionnaire, 3e Régiment Étranger d'Infanterie; Algeria, 1960

E

1: Commandant, 4e Régiment Étranger Quartier Capitaine Danjou, Castelnaudary, France, 1980s
2: Drum sergeant, Musique Principale; Summer parade dress, Paris, Bastille Day, mid-1980s
3: Caporal-chef, 13e Demi-Brigade de la Légion Étrangère, tropical guard dress; Quartier Montclar, Djibouti, late 1980s

F

1: Légionnaire 1ère classe, 1er Régiment Étranger de Cavalerie, Winter walking-out dress; Quartier Labouche, Orange, France, late 1980s

2: Légionnaire 1ère classe, section LMG gunner, 1ère Compagnie, 2e Régiment Étranger d'Infanterie; Operation Épervier, Abéché, Chad, 1989

3: Légionnaire 1ère classe, platoon radio operator, 3e Compagnie, 13e Demi-Brigade de la Légion Étrangère; Djibouti, late 1980s

G

1: Caporal, 6e Régiment Étranger de Genie; As Salman, Iraq, February 1991
2: Tireur d'élite, 3e Compagnie, 2e Régiment Étranger d'Infanterie; UNPROFOR, Bosnia, Summer 1993
3: Légionnaire 1ère classe, mortar platoon, Compagnie d'Éclairage et d'Appui, 2e Régiment Étranger d'Infanterie; IFOR, Bosnia 1995
4: Brigadier, 3e Escadron, 1er Régiment Étranger de Cavalerie; IFOR, Bosnia, February 1996

1

2

3

4

The M8 was retained throughout the war by the armoured car platoons of the motorised intervention regiments; this is probably a 4e REI crew near Guelma behind the Morice Line in January 1960. Note green beret with first type grenade badge – see under Plate E4. (Courtesy Wayne Braby)

Chellala. On Moroccan border 1961; Tlemcen, Jan.1962. By ceasefire, 146 dead, 353 wounded.

6e REI

Former Legion garrison regiment in the Levant, disbanded after resisting 1941 Allied invasion of Syria, re-formed in Tunisia 1947 as reception/transit pool for Indochina drafts. 1954-55, single remaining battalion on ops. against Tunisian insurgents. Disbanded June 1955.

13e DBLE

Three battalions landed Bizerta and Algiers, June-July 1955. Ops. on Tunisian border, Guelma, Philippeville, the Nementchas; 1956, III/13e

The classic desert patrol truck was the Dodge 6x6. This photo shows a platoon of a CSPL, probably the 3e at Ft. Leclerc in the Fezzan; most of the men wear the traditional Saharan Y-shaped red leather bandolier equipment.

disbanded. 1957-58, ops. in the Aurès. Oct.1958, became intervention regiment; ops. all over eastern Algeria 1958-59, based Batna, then Bougie. Op. Étincelles, in Hodna massif; Op. Jumelles, Kabylia; Pierres Précieuses, Philippeville, Collo Peninsula. Jan.-March 1960 in Algiers, thence to Tunisian frontier. 1961-62, ops. Morice Line, Kabylia, Aurès; at March 1962 ceasefire opposite 'Duck's Beak' of Tunisian frontier. 159 men killed or died of wounds.

***Légionnaire* of the 4e CSPL wearing the traditional Saharan leather equipment in reddened leather. Note his company badge: all Saharan unit insignia were based on this 'Agades cross'**

1er REC

1er GA landed Mers-el-Kebir, Nov.1955-Feb.1956; to Sousse, Tunisia; reorganised as four sqns., March 1956. Ops. S Tunisia, SE Algeria, 1956; Dec. to Bou-Saada, Algeria. 1957, ops. S Algeria; April, M8 armoured cars replaced by French Panhards; Oct., 4e Esc. disbanded. May 1958, to Tebessa; Tunisian border patrols. 1959, to Batna; ops. in the Aurès, Nementchas; 1960, ops. S Constantine province – elements fought as motorised or heli-mobile infantry as appropriate. April 1961, some personnel suspected of involvement in 'Generals' Putsch'; Aug., to W Algeria – Marnia, Saida; at Tlemcen March 1962. Total casualties 45 killed, 150 wounded.

2e REC

Oct.1955, absorbed 1er REC's 2^{e} GA on return from Indochina as 4^{e} Escadron. Crossed from Morocco to Algeria, summer 1956; to Ouargla, Touggourt, Ghardaia, Laghouat in deep south. Aug.1956, 2e Esc. detached to 1er REP for Suez operation, later retained. 1957, ops.south central region; unit maintained large element motorised infantry. Spring 1958, two sqns. to Négrine, southern sector Morice Line; Dec.1958, regt. to Djelfa; ops. south central region 1959-60. 1961, to southern bases; Feb.1962, south Aurès, Biskra, Négrine. Total casualties, 56 dead, 98 wounded.

The CSPLs

The Compagnies Sahariennes Portées de la Légion were deep-desert patrol companies, in the tradition of the old Compagnies Méharistes, equipped with patrol trucks and a small armoured car element. Active throughout the Algerian War, they assured the security of the trans-continental roads and the oases dotted along them; of the important French oilfields in the far south; and of the cross-border caravan routes far to the south of the defended frontier lines, which the ALN sometimes attempted to use for infiltration. In high summer they tended to move north, taking part in combined operations with the intervention units. They were highly mobile and self-sufficient, moving like nomads over huge distances between widely dispersed bases.

The 1ère CSPL dated from March 1946, when the single CSPLE split into the 1ère and 2e CSPLs. Based at various times at Ain-Sefra, Fort Flatters, Laghouat and Reggane, it was redesignated *1er Escadron SPL* – taking cavalry ranks and uniform distinctions, but with unchanged vehicles – in Jan.1961. The 2e CSPL was stationed at Ouargla and Laghouat. The 3e CSPL was formed in Feb.1949 and based at Fort Leclerc (Sebha) in the Fezzan, the Libyan border region. The 4e CSPL was formed in Jan.1956 from the former 24e CPLE of the GPLE d'Algérie, and was stationed at Colomb-Béchar.

The Algerian War cost the Foreign Legion a total of 65 officers and 1,911 enlisted men killed in action or died of wounds.

The breast badge – in silver with green/red sidestripes – has remained unchanged during the progression from the DCRE of 1945 to today's COMLE.

Central Administration

The French Foreign Legion's organisational relationship to the rest of the French Army resembles that of the British Brigade of Guards rather than that of the United States Marine Corps. The several regiments of the Legion enjoy a collective identity administratively and traditionally, but have never been grouped for operational purposes in exclusively Foreign Legion formations, always serving side by side with other French units in common subordination to higher commands.

The unifying administrative level in 1945 was the *Dépôt Commun des Régiments Étrangers (DCRE)*, with recruitment, training and personnel responsibilities, and commanded by a senior colonel. In 1948 Gen. Montclar was appointed *Inspecteur de la Légion Étrangère*; in this capacity he was to advise the Ministry of War and the General Staff on all matters specific to the Legion. There followed a complex series of changes to the title and exact scope of the unifying entity; but in 1972 many of the duties and prerogatives of an Inspector were resumed, in fact if not in name, when Gen. Letestu was appointed to command the *Groupement de la Légion Étrangère (GLE)*. 1984 saw the recreation, in effect, of the old Inspectorate under the title *Commandement de la Légion Étrangère*, headed by a general officer with the title of *Commandant*, responsible for the administration, welfare, morale, personnel management and training of all Legion units, and for representing the Legion at all levels.

THE DIASPORA

Foreign Legion organisation and deployment since 1962

The aftermath of the Algerian War was perhaps the unhappiest period in the Legion's history. Although only one regiment had taken part in the April 1961 'Generals' Putsch', numbers of former légionnaires had joined the OAS (Secret Army Organisation). This terrorist group waged a continuing campaign of atrocity both in Algeria – in an attempt to destabilise the preparations for independence – and in France itself, making several determined attempts on the life of President de Gaulle. A febrile atmosphere of guilt by association cast into some doubt the future of the whole corps. Some held that with the loss of Algeria the Legion's *raison d'être* had passed into history, and that a mercenary corps had no place in France's post-colonial army. By the time the residual Algerian bases were given up most Legion units had been reduced or widely dispersed.

1er RE

Left the historic base at Sidi-bel-Abbes for the last time in Oct.1962, and moved to the new *maison mère* being built at Aubagne near Marseilles.

Currently at Quartier Viennot, Aubagne. The central depot unit, tasked with recruitment, selection and induction, personnel management, and a wide range of central services. In wartime, contributes detachments to 6e and/or 14e DLB.

Foreign Legion Services Co. (CSLE); Command & Regimental Services Co. (CCSR); Foreign Legion Personnel Administration Co. (CAPLE); Foreign Legion Transit Co. (CTLE); Principal Band; Pioneers.

3e REI, Souk-Ahras, April 1961. At the climax of the Algerian War the camouflaged '*tenue léopard*' dominated French military fashion, and units started to add their parade embellishments to this combat uniform rather than turning out in service dress. Note here the triple *fourragère*, regimental badge, and Presidental Unit Citation ribbon; many photos show epaulettes and blue sashes worn with camouflage fatigues. (Courtesy Charles Milassin)

2e REI

Concentrated at Colomb-Béchar in Oct.1962 as main residual garrison for French Saharan concessionary areas. Absorbed 1er ESPL and 4e CSPL, April 1963, and remnant of 4e REI, April 1964. Moved into Mers-el-Kebir base area, late 1967; disbanded Jan.1968, except for single Cie. de Marche, which in Aug.1968 was the last Legion unit to leave Algeria. Re-formed as 2e RE Sept.1972 at Corte and Bonifacio, Corsica, comprising Groupement d'Instruction and Groupement Operationelle de la Légion Étrangère (GILE & GOLE). GILE, with four companies, carried out all basic and most specialist training of Legion recruits; GOLE was an air-portable infantry combat force with HQ and three companies. In Oct.1976 basic training moved to Castelnaudary in France, a new Régiment d'Instruction (RILE) inheriting the lineage of the old 4e REI.

Resumed title 2e REI, June 1980; 1981-84 operationally subordinate to 31e Brigade, an element of the FAR (Rapid Action Force), while retaining a specialist training role. During this period it comprised HQ & Services Company; Recce & Support Company; 5^{e} & 6^{e} Cies., respectively specialising in amphibious and mountain tactics and incorporating Milan ATGW, mortar and 20mm AA cannon sections as well as infantry

Algeria, c.1960: the introduction of the all-arms fatigues was gradual. Here a man of the motorised units, eating off what looks like the tailgate of an old Dodge Command Car, wears a camouflage para jump smock with M1947 green fatigue trousers and 'rangers'. (Courtesy Wayne Braby)

platoons; 7e Cie., specialising in helicopter and night fighting tactics; and Cie. d'Instruction des Spécialistes. Since returning from Lebanon in 1984, stationed at Nîmes, southern France, subordinate to 6e Division Légère Blindé, FAR.

Currently at Quartier Vallongue, Nîmes. Armoured infantry/light anti-tank regiment (92 x VAB wheeled APCs, 1,200 men).

HQ & Services Co. (CCS); Recce & Support Co. (CEA) – 12 x 120mm mortar, 24 x Milan ATGW, 10 x 20mm AA cannon; four numbered rifle companies.

The Legion rifle company typically has an HQ and four platoons, each platoon of three ten-man squads. The squad, led by an NCO, is divided into two assault or fire teams; it is armed with FAMAS rifles (plus 58mm AP and AT rifle grenades), one FR F-2 sniper's rifle with scope sights, one LRAC 89mm rocket launcher and, depending upon deployment, may have one AA.52 belt-fed machine gun. In European theatres the 120mm APILAS rocket launcher is also issued at squad level.

Orange, 1976: although the Legion had lost its African home, it still had men of the old school. This grizzled *brigadier-chef* of the 1er REC wears the coveted Medaille Militaire for gallantry, and medals for World War II, Indochina and Algeria. These do not tie up with his three re-enlistment chevrons, which would give him a maximum of 20 years' service. He probably served, under more than one name, for far longer than officially permitted (the Legion could sometimes be human in such cases); at any rate, in 1979 he was photographed parading with the 4^{e} Esc. sporting no less than five re-enlistment chevrons, which is legally impossible. (ECPA)

3^{e} REI

Shipped from Algeria to Diego-Suarez, Madagascar, in 1963, remaining until Sept.1973. It was then transferred to Guyane (French Guiana) on the north-east coast of South America.

Currently at Quartier Forget, Kourou, Guyane; Camp Szuts, Regina, Guyane. Motorised light infantry regiment tasked with security of Kourou Space Centre; running Equatorial Forest Training Centre (CEFE); and regional security. Subordinate to Forces Armées aux Antilles-Guyane.

CCS; CEA – scout ptn., 20mm AA ptn., 81mm mortar ptn., engineer ptn.; 2e Cie. – rifle co. tasked with base defence, sniper training, local recce in 'ultra-lite' aircraft; 3e Cie. – rifle co. tasked with riverine ops., close combat training. During space launches a third rifle co., not necessarily Legion, attached temporarily.

4^{e} REI/RE

Moved July 1962 to southern Algerian oilfields and nuclear facility; absorbed 2^{e} and 3^{e} CSPLs, April 1963. Disbanded April 1964, remaining effectives passing to 2^{e} REI. Sept.1977, new RILE (see 2^{e} REI above) formed at Castelnaudary, inheriting lineage of 4^{e} REI; retitled in June 1980 as 4^{e} RE.

Currently at Quartier Danjou, Castelnaudary. Tasked with all Legion basic, NCO, technical and specialist training; subordinate to COMLE; in wartime, reinforces 14^{e} DLB. Basic training, including instruction in French language, lasts 16 weeks. Promising candidates may progress to further nine weeks training for corporal, then 15 weeks for sergeant.

CCS; NCO Training Co. (CIC); Specialist Training Co. (CIS) – signals, medics, drivers, etc.; 1st, 2nd, 3rd Volunteer Training Cos. (CEVs).

5e REI/RE

Based Colomb-Béchar, Ain-Sefra after 1962 ceasefire; warned in March 1963 for transfer to Tahiti, French Polynesia; officially disbanded at Mers-el-Kebir, lineage passing to newly raised 5e Régiment Mixte du Pacifique, incorporating both Legion and army Engineer elements. First 5e RMP personnel shipped to Tahiti June 1963; Sept., first detachment

Aubagne, 1965: 1ère Section [platoon], 1ère Compagnie, 1er RE in parade dress. Note the NCO *port-fanion* in the foreground, with a second, gold-trimmed chinstrap worn down; although he seems to be a *sergent-chef* his *képi* is covered for this parade. The small company flag is flown from a staff which fits into the rifle muzzle. (ECPA)

to Muroroa Atoll to begin construction of nuclear test facility, where HQ transferred Jan.1976. July 1984 retitled 5e RE.

Currently at Centre d'Expérimentations du Pacifique (CEP), Mururoa Atoll; periodic detachments to other islands; transit camp at Arue, Tahiti. Tasked with construction and maintenance of infrastructure, vehicle maintenance, local and regional security. Subordinate to CEP.

CCS; Engineer Co. (CG); Combat & Heavy Works Co. (CCT); Transport & Maintenance Co.(CTR).

6e REG

Currently at Quartier General Rollet (Camp St Maurice l'Ardoise), Laudun, southern France. Motorised/armoured combat engineer regiment, subordinate to 6e DLB. 6e Régiment Étranger de Génie formed July 1984, inheriting lineage of former 6e REI 'Régiment of the Levant'; tasked with obstacle building and clearance, mine laying and clearance, sabotage, river & beach recce, light bridging. (Note: during 1970s-80s mixed army Engineer/Foreign Legion construction unit, 61e Bn.Mixte Génie-Légion, was based at Canjuers, southern France.)

CCS – includes bridging ptn.; Support Co. (CA) – includes DINOPS ptn., multi-mission para/scuba-qualified recce & combat divers comparable to US Navy SEALs; 1st, 2nd & 3rd Assault Engineer Cos. (VABs, MPGs plus various specialist vehicles).

13e DBLE

Transferred April-Oct.1962 to Djibouti, strategic French military base in 'Horn of Africa' (then, officially, the Territory of the Affars and Issas).

Currently at Quartier Montclar, Republic of Djibouti.

Multi-role motorised regiment tasked with local/regional security, and/or overseas intervention; runs Arta Beach Commando Training Centre (CECAP). Subordinate to Forces Francaises/Djibouti (FFDj).

HQ, Support & Services Co. (CCAS) – includes Milan ATGW & 120mm mortar ptns.; 2nd/Works Co. (2e CT) – construction co., bulldozers etc.; 3rd/Rifle Co. (3e Cie.) – motorised in VLRA patrol trucks, ptns. also trained in specialist roles, respectively recce diving, demolition, sniping; integral Recce Sqn. – 12 x ERC-90 Sagaie armoured cars, VLRA ptn. (Note: a rotating company of the 2e REP is often attached.)

1er REC

March 1962-Jan.1964, based Mecheria; then to Mers-el-Kebir. Shipped Oct.1967 to Orange, southern France.

Currently at Quartier Labouche, Orange.

Armoured recce/anti-tank regiment, subordinate to 6e DLB. Main equipment AMX-10RC 6x6 heavy armoured car, four crew, 105mm gun, cross-country mobility comparable to tracked armour, unprepared amphibious capability.

HQ & Services Sqn.(ECS); 1er, 2e & 3e Esc. – each 12 x AMX-10RC; 4e Esc. – 12 x VCAC/HOT with quad HOT2 ATGWs.

2e REC

Disbanded July 1962, remaining effectives absorbed by 1er REC.

DLEM

Established 1967, as DLEC, by rotating companies from 3e REI on Madagascar, Détachement de la Légion Étrangère en Mayotte now based

In the early 1970s the REC replaced the heavy eight-wheeled armoured car with the 4.5-ton, three-man Panhard AML; typically each troop had two AML-90 gun cars (left) and two AML-60 mortar cars. It was with this equipment that the 1er Escadron saw combat in Chad in Spring 1978 during Operation Tacaud. (ECPA)

Camerone Day in the new Quartier Vienot, Aubagne: the holy moment of the Legion's year. On 30 April 1970 the 1er RE parade before the Monument to the Dead, carefully transported from Sidi-bel-Abbes. At left, escorted by NCOs carrying the company *fanions*, a decorated Legion veteran carries the casket holding the wooden hand of Capitaine Danjou, killed at Camerone in Mexico on 30 April 1863. (ECPA)

Dzaoudzi, Mayotte, Comoro Islands; maintains French presence in strategic Mozambique Channel; subordinate to Forces Armées/ Zone Sud de l'Ocean Indien (FAZSOI).

HQ & Services Co., plus rotating company from either Legion or Airborne. 1984, inherited standard of 2e REC.

During the late 1960s and 1970s it became clear that France's overseas military commitments, while less demanding in numbers and more fragmented, would not disappear. Foreign policy demands that French influence be maintained in her former African colonies; and this influence rests ultimately on her willingness to deploy troops in support of allies and in protection of French interests. The bulk of the French army were short-term conscripts fulfilling a military training commitment inadequate for the creation of effective intervention units with sophisticated modern equipment. Apart from the relatively small career element grouped in the Marine (former Colonial) and Airborne regiments, the Legion has represented the only available pool of combat-ready professional infantry. (A cynic might reflect that in these sometimes ambiguous adventures it does no harm to use units at least half of whose members are not related to French voters...)

In the late 1960s a growing recognition that a new and rewarding role might be within the grasp of the demoralised Foreign Legion gave birth to a whole new style, pioneered by the paras of the 2^{e} REP but soon embraced by the other combat units. Historically the Legion had provided old-fashioned heavy infantry, to take and hold colonies; for the 1970s-80s the emphasis would be on flexibility, rapid mobility, multiple skills, new equipment and new tactics. Large overseas garrisons would be replaced by small, hard-hitting forces dispersed to strategic points as regional 'fire brigades'. These would be regularly supplemented by units rotating through from France for field training; and could be deployed and reinforced by air at short notice in case of regional unrest. At the same time, the heavy core units of the Legion – 2e REI and 1er REC – would be fully integrated into the French line of battle facing the Iron Curtain in Europe.

Chad

The former colony which has most often called for French military assistance is the Republic of Chad, a fly-blown, chronically ill-governed, but strategic expanse of the Saharan desert fringe south of Libya. In April-September 1969 France sent in the 2e REP, in the Legion's first combat deployment since Algeria, to support the Tombalbaye regime against insurgents. They were reinforced in September by a motorised Compagnie de Marche drawn from the Legion's non-airborne units (CMLE). The Legion was withdrawn by December 1970, after suffering about a dozen killed in brisk skirmishes during successful motorised patrols.

During the 1970s-80s Legion paras and armour returned to Chad several times, as part of larger French deployments, to fight or deter both FROLINAT insurgents and, from 1973, Libyan troops after President Gadaffi annexed the mineral-rich Aouzou Strip. During periodic coups bringing Presidents Maloum, Habre and Deby to power, French troops remained aloof. In May 1978 (Operation Tacaud) 1er Esc./1er REC, with AML-90 and -60 armoured cars, saw action against Libyan-backed rebels at Salal, Ati and Djedda, later patrolling a tolerated demarkation zone. 4e Esc.(Porté) arrived in June 1979, 3e Esc. in August; and 2e Esc. to replace 1er in September, when the unit withdrew. A more ambitious Libyan/FROLINAT push in June 1983 brought the largest French deployment yet (Operation Manta), including 2e/1er REC by September. After three years of relative calm on the 'Red Line' the re-formed Chadian forces (FANT) struck north, backed by major French reinforcements including the 1er REC (Operation Épervier). Without help from French ground combat units, FANT wiped out Libyan armour in brigade strength at Bir-Kora and Wadi Doum on 19-22 March 1987. Companies/squadrons of the 2e REP, 1er REC, 2e REI and 6e REG continue to rotate through Chad on temporary deployments.

Each Legion regiment has a pioneer section, that of the 1er RE being the largest; they play a large part in ceremonial, often parading with the central band at public events. They are traditionally bearded, and parade with leather aprons and felling axes; note also the crossed axes motif on the *écusson* on this *capo-chef's* right sleeve, balancing the Legion grenade patch on the left. (EPCA)

Other African active service deployments

During the prolonged wars in Somalia and Ethiopia in the 1960s-80s the 13e DBLE and rotating companies in Djibouti sometimes clashed with various forces during frontier patrols, the term 'frontier' often being robustly interpreted. The only incident widely reported was the seizure by Somali terrorists in February 1976 of 31 children in a Djiboutian school bus, which was driven to Loyada on the Somali border. Recce Sqn./13e DBLE took part in the successful rescue operation (together with 2e/2e REP), and returned the fire of Somali troops covering the terrorists from across the frontier.

Saudi Arabia, January 1991: men of the 2e REI prepare to advance on the left flank of the Coalition offensive, wearing green C86 NBC suits and the new desert-camouflage covers on their helmets and body armour – see also Plate H1. The corporal at left carries a radio, the squad sniper in the centre the 7.5mm FR F1 rifle with 3.8x L806 scope. (ECPA)

In May-June 1990 a company each from the 2e REI and 2e REP were flown to Gabon when anti-government rioters seized European hostages at Port Gentil; the hostages were later released after negotiation.

Operation Baumier in Zaire in February 1991 saw 3e/2e REI driving over the border from the French base at Bangui, Central African Republic, to Kinshasa to protect and evacuate foreign nationals during a period of bloodshed; the 1er/2e REI was also flown in.

The appalling Hutu and Tutsi tribal massacres which drew the world's horrified attention to Rwanda in 1994 prompted the despatch of French units in an attempt to create protected zones, including elements of the 2e REI and 3e/13e DBLE.

Beirut, June 1983-March 1984

Following the Sabra/Chatilla atrocities the Western powers sent the second Multi-National Force to the Lebanese capital to hold the ceasefire line while negotiations proceeded. Alongside US, Italian and British troops the reinforced French 31e Brigade arrived in June 1983 (Operation Diodon III) with the 2e REI (CCS, CEA, 5e, 6e and 7e Cies.); a tactical HQ and two squadrons of the 1er REC, who were flown in without vehicles and took over AML-90s already in-country; and the brigade advanced HQ (ECSI) whose protection platoon was drawn from the 1er and 4e REs. The légionnaires carried out their delicate mission with notable restraint; and lost some half a dozen dead in the process.

The Gulf War, 1991

The French ground contribution to the Coalition, designated Division Daguet, was essentially the 6e DLB much reinforced. The first to arrive at Yanbu, Saudi Arabia, in September 1990 were the 2e REI. The 1er REC, 2e REI and most of the 6e REG provided, with the 1er Spahis, the western axis of the division's advance into Iraq with US XVIII Airborne Corps units on 24 February 1991 (3e Cie./6e REG was with the eastern axis, largely of Marine units). In fact men of 2e REI and 6e REG had penetrated 5km into Iraq on the night of 22 February to take 'Natchez', an Iraqi post dominating their line of advance up an escarpment; the légionnaire-sappers and US 1/27th Engineers built a track up the escarpment on the 23rd. The French columns – the most westerly, screening the Coalition left flank – punched through the Iraqi 45th Division with considerable ease, and took their objective – the town and airfield of As Salman – by the morning of the 26th; some 3,000 Iraqi prisoners were taken. There were no Legion casualties.

Bosnia, 1993-96

From the first deployment of UN troops to Bosnia the French made the largest contribution, maintaining in the Sarajevo sector at least two infantry battalions assembled from rotating companies from various units of the 11^{e} DP, 9^{e} DM and 6^{e} DLB together with support and service units. Legion paras and elements from the 2^{e} REI, 1er REC and 6^{e} REG have frequently staged through these task force units, and continue to do so now that the UNPROFOR has been replaced by the IFOR under NATO rather than UN command; the transitional period during which the Serbian siege of Sarajevo was raised saw the entire 2^{e} REI deployed around Mt. Igman. Casualties have been suffered; the losses inflicted on local snipers are not officially known. In this murderous arena all Western troops have so far conducted themselves with commendable self-discipline under provocation; but any deliberate incoming fire is returned until decisively silenced.

Bosnia, March 1996: troopers of the 3e Esc./1er REC on patrol in a Panhard VBL 4x4 amphibious light armoured vehicle. Their practical but anonymous camouflaged fatigues and body armour are set off by the *képi blanc* – characteristically, the Legion wish all comers to know exactly who they are. (Carl Schulze)

The Legion Today

The Legion's diminished size (currently 8,000-9,000 men), and the mass unemployment and political upheavals of the past 15 years have provided a steady flow of recruits which has allowed a selective enlistment policy – it has been claimed that seven out of every ten applicants are turned away, in favour of the youngest, fittest, most intelligent and best-motivated. Even so, the 4^{e} RE processes some 1,700 recruits annually. Conditions of service, career prospects, pay and allowances have improved out of all recognition since the years when the Legion was a neglected repository for colonial cannon-fodder. Five years' honourable service will still bring a foreigner French citizenship; and the inducements to re-enlist are attractive, giving the Legion a strong corps of experienced career NCOs. The ambiguous relationship between France and her Foreign Legion in the early 1960s is now long forgotten. The corps today enjoys great prestige once again; and with the announcement in early 1996 that France intended to move towards a wholly professional army at the turn of the century, the Legion's future seems assured.

THE PLATES

Heavily dependent on foreign supplies for several years, the CEFEO made do with what was available: largely US and British surplus, supplemented by some pre-war French matériel, and later by French-made copies of Allied models. It would be the early 1950s before standardisation on new French designs even began to be achieved; old items would survive in isolated cases surprisingly late, as did a lively individualism born of the need to improvise in the 1940s. It is therefore impossible to generalise from the particular; almost until the end of the Algerian War individual regiments might display 'tribal' differences.

Given the limitations of space, we have selected examples of the main types of uniform during the main periods of active service. The disproportionate number of junior NCOs illustrated offer the best 'value for space' in terms of visual information on enlisted ranks' uniforms generally. We have not duplicated a number of subjects covered – with unit differences only – in Elite 6, *French Foreign Legion Paratroops*, particularly from the period c.1962-1980. Equally, we have omitted all but passing mention of unit breast badges – a vast subject, published at length elsewhere. The figures in these plates are either copied from individual photographs, or are composites combining – to give optimum information – features from more than one photographed figure from the same period and unit.

In these notes we have used the British rather than the US terms for colours: i.e. 'khaki' here means the drab brown – US 'olive drab' – used for woollen uniforms (in French, *tenues de drap*); and 'khaki drill' the pale yellowish tan – US 'khaki' – used for lightweight summer/tropical dress (in French, *tenues de toile* – the heavier material used for combat fatigues is termed in French *treillis de combat*). For consistency the style e.g. 'M1947' indicates the designation date of equipment of all nationalities.

French non-commissioned ranks are conventionally grouped into *troupes* – troops, from *soldat* to *caporal-chef*: *sous-officiers* – NCOs, from *sergent* to *sergent-major*; and *adjudants* – warrant officers, from *adjudant* to *major*. The uniform distinctions of *caporal-chef* have wandered, according to unit and period, between those worn by troops and by NCOs. We have used italic type only for French ranks or specific terms for uniform items.

A1: Maréchal-des-logis, 1er Régiment Étranger de Cavalerie; Austria, spring 1945 Although this cavalry sergeant preparing for a march-past wears almost entirely US issue (M1939 OD wool service dress, OD wool shirt, light OD tie, M1936 web pistol belt and suspenders, SMG magazine pouches, M1938 dismounted leggings, M1943 'flesh-out' service shoes), he typifies the Legion's determination to cling to whatever 'tribal' items they could lay hands on. *Képis* were in short supply; he wears the midnight blue (virtually black) and red M1927/35 troops' model, with red applique Legion grenade badge, its white cover removed to mark *sous-officier* status – his rank entitles him to a silver grenade badge, but this is better than nothing. In 1943 the Legion's arm of service badge became a midnight blue diamond-shaped *écusson* edged with triple green piping, bearing the Legion grenade in green for troops and infantry

BELOW **Dien Bien Phu, spring 1954: a wounded officer of I/2e REI (identified by a veteran as 'Lt. Boissy'), wearing khaki drill shirt with – unusually in the field – the full M1946 shoulderboards of rank; and M1947 green fatigue trousers with, just visible tucked in the right side of the belt, a green/red sidecap with added grenade badge. Detail photos show an officer's shoulderboard, midnight blue with green chevrons and gold grenade, here with captain's three gold *galons*; and 'banana' sidecap, green with red top fold, added warrant officer's rank lace, non-regulation gold grenade and front buttons.**

gold or cavalry silver for NCOs, worn on the left sleeve immediately below any rank chevrons. Supplies were inadequate before the late 1940s, however; and this NCO has improvised with an M1926 tunic collar *écusson*, with double piping at the top two edges only. He has found silver cavalry buttons for his tunic; and has quickly secured the new *fourragère* or lanyard (marking a regiment's two or three citations in Army orders) worn on the left shoulder – in the colours of the Croix de Guerre 1914-18 but distinguished by an 'olive' above the ferrule in the colours of the C de G 1939-40. This veteran has also managed to retain the metal regimental badge dating from 1936, worn pinned to his right breast pocket; and the Legion's traditional dark blue parade sash. It would be 1947 before the 1er REC gave up the pale khaki necktie for the green tie, first taken from *Chantiers de Jeunesse* stocks and worn with walking-out dress by the RMLE in 1944. Photos of this date show submachine-guns (usually the Thompson M1928A1 or M1A1) carried by NCOs only.

A2: Adjudant, Régiment de Marche de la Légion Étrangère / Extreme Orient; Oran, 10 February 1946 The RMLE/EO (redesignated 2e REI while still en route) were issued complete British woollen battledress uniforms and webbing equipment three days before embarking on the *Cameronia* for Indochina. The original photo shows a group similarly dressed, equipped and armed (with the Lee-Enfield .303 No.4); most wear the white-covered M1927 *képi*, but this *adjudant* has a scarlet and green sidecap. This *calot* was first issued, largely due to the wartime shortage of *képis*, during the 1943 re-equipment in North Africa, and in these colours was originally specific to the wartime RMLE. In Indochina it was sometimes worn as an alternative barracks and working headgear by all ranks of Legion infantry units, in three styles: the regulation rectangular type copied from the US Army overseas cap, with a diagonal fold at the front right of the turn-up; the taller and more curved 'Colonial' style (see Plate C1), which shared this feature; and this privately purchased 'banana' style, more sharply curved and with a shallower turn-up front and rear, which lacked the fold. This warrant officer has added the single red-flecked silver lace of his rank to the front body of the cap in a chevron, officer-style. It was perhaps unusual to see a warrant officer armed with a rifle, but the photo is clear; this was probably due to the very recent issue of new equipment. The French M1931 colonial helmet was issued before embarkation and is seen in some photos attached to the M1908 'large pack'.

A3: Sergent, 2e Régiment Étranger d'Infanterie; post garrison, Annam, c.1950 In 1946-50 British and US clothing was almost universal: for hot weather barracks, walking-out and local combat dress, either the British khaki drill Aertex shirt (less frequently the four-pocket bush jacket) and ample cotton shorts or long trousers (the former usually rolled and stitched or cut shorter); or the US khaki shade 1 'chino' long-sleeved shirt (both with and without shoulder straps) and matching trousers or shorts. Photos show these worn alongside the French M1936 sand-khaki short-sleeved shirt and shorts, and later M1946 long-sleeved khaki drill shirt and slacks. This NCO, typically equipped for a routine morning road-opening patrol, wears the French M1931 colonial helmet; British shirt and shorts; British M1937 skeleton webbing including paired cartridge carriers and pistol case; one of the locally made SMG pouches quite commonly seen, used here for Sten magazines; and the

ABOVE **M1946 *képi* for officers and warrant officers, here for an infantry *adjudant-chef*: black body, red crown, all gold lace except for single horizontal *galon* around top of body, which for this rank is gold flecked with tiny red chevrons. The *adjudant* wears the same but in red-flecked silver; in the cavalry the precedence is reversed.**

popular French canvas and rubber tropical ankle boots (called 'baskets', or *pataugas* – 'splashers'). The helmet bears a locally made brass badge of the Legion grenade with red/green enamelled bomb. The Legion's 1943 *écusson* is worn on the left upper sleeve; some early examples show only these small triple green chevrons above the grenade rather than full edging. The double gold chevron of an infantry sergeant was worn on the left sleeve only, immediately above the *écusson*, before 1948; thereafter all rank chevrons were ordered worn on both arms, but in casual uniform a single left sleeve array remained common.

B1: Légionnaire, 13e Demi-Brigade de la Légion Étrangère; Cochinchina, 1948-50 This man wears a US Army 'chino' shirt (here an officer's type with shoulder straps) and matching shorts; the US leggings are worn over French leather M1917 *brodequins*. For local operations the necessary minimum of equipment was carried and infantry often wore only belt order; here we see the US M1923 cartridge belt, M1936 suspenders, field dressing pouch and two-pocket grenade pouch, and a slung British water bottle.

ABOVE LEFT **Field ranking for *lieutenant-colonel*; the bi-metal clip was popular in Algeria, often replacing the gold/silver braid on black usually seen in Indochina. (Courtesy Chris Barbarski)** CENTRE **M1946 troops' shoulderboard, midnight blue with all green embroidery.** RIGHT ***Epaulette de tradition* in emerald green and scarlet, here with gold thread edging and barring the crescent to mark *sous-officier* rank.**

Like most units, the 13ᵉ carried at this period a mixture of small arms: photos show this .30 cal. M1903 Springfield rifle as standard, alongside the .30 cal. M1 carbine, .45 cal. M1928A1 or M1A1 Thompson, and .303 Bren LMG. For lack of anything better French infantry were also widely issued with the French M1931A2 Reibel, a machine gun designed for tank and fortress mounting and awkwardly adapted to an infantry tripod.

The 13ᵉ DBLE were proud of their distinction as the only Legion unit to fight on the Allied side throughout World War II, and this man wears the khaki wool beret, originally pre-war French Army fortress troops' issue but worn by the 13ᵉ for the Narvik campaign in 1940, and retained (or improvised) as field headgear whenever possible until the late 1950s – often pulled right in the British style. He also carries slung round his neck the French khaki drill bush hat which spread rapidly throughout the Expeditionary Corps from 1949. Photos show some men of the 13ᵉ wearing their metal regimental breast badge on operations.

B2: Legion infantryman; Tonkin, 1950-54 During this period a degree of standardisation was achieved in clothing, though never in personal equipment and weapons. The bush hat became universal; although US M1 helmets were widely issued they were carried slung whenever possible. The French M1947 *treillis* or *tenue de campagne* was now becoming the standard combat dress; note four internal jacket pockets with pointed external flaps, two large leg pockets, buttoned tabs at wrist and ankle, and concealed buttons – here the legs are tabbed at the ankle over *pataugas*. The French web equipment designated M1950 *type TAP* – 'airborne troops type' – was slow to reach Legion infantry, and a mixture of US, British, and French webbing remained in use; this man wears all US items. His dagger is a cut-down M1886 Lebel bayonet; and he carries French OF37 'offensive' blast grenades, although US fragmentation grenades were also widely used. His rifle is the standard French type from before World War II until the late 1950s: the 7.5mm MAS.36, with a five-round fixed magazine, which had largely replaced foreign rifles by the second half of the war, although the M1 carbine remained common.

B3: Section light machine-gunner, Legion infantry; Tonkin, 1950-54 Until nearly 1960 the standard French section light machine-gun was the 7.5mm FM.24/29. This gunner wears the US M1 helmet with netting, French M1947 fatigues, M1917 boots, and M1945 canvas anklets – copied from the British type but with only one strap and an internal tongue-and-pocket fastening at the bottom corner. His equipment is based on the French *TAP* M1950 belt and suspenders. His 'all-arms musette M1950' is attached to the suspenders by the same system as the British M1908 pack. He carries slung the smaller of two types of FM.24/29 magazine pouch. His belt order is typically mixed: British M1944 canteen in a French M1950 carrier, British M1937 universal pouch retained for FM.24/29 accessories, pre-war leather case for the LMG cleaning rod, and a French billhook.

The next plate illustrates just some of the further variety of clothing seen in Indochina:

C1: Lieutenant-Colonel Charton; RC.4, October 1950 The commander of the doomed column retreating from Cao Bang – and formerly of III/2ᵉ REI – was photographed wearing the 'Colonial'-shaped *bonnet de police* or *calot* in Legion colours. As with the black braid slides on his shoulder straps, Lt.Col. Charton's cap bears the five rank *galons* of (gold/silver/gold/space/silver/gold). He wears the British 'jungle green' tropical battledress blouse, and British khaki drill slacks.

C2: Légionnaire, 2e Compagnie, I/3e Régiment Étranger d'Infanterie; Phu Tong Hoa, 27 July 1948 Lt.Col. Simon's account, and the few indistinct photos, suggest that the guard mounted to greet him put on *képis*, sashes, and the regiment's contemporary double *fourragère* (Légion d'Honneur & Croix de Guerre 1914-18 with various 'olives', inherited from the wartime RMLE) worn in the walking-out position rather than taken across to the top shirt button in parade style. At least one regimental pocket badge may be made out in the photos. This figure wears the French M1946 khaki drill shirt, US surplus 'chino' slacks, and the French pre-war belt; scrubbed British M1937 belts and anklets were also seen among the garrison. The *képi* is the M1946 type, with a white drawstring cover of a shape devised by the wartime RMLE and which saw some use in Indochina.

C3: Sergent, II/2e Régiment Étranger d'Infanterie; Laos, April 1954 Note 1952 'lightened' version of the M1947 fatigue shirt, with breast pockets only, doubled shoulder yoke reinforcement and buttoned cuffs, made in the same olive croise coton 320 material as the four-pocket version and worn tucked into the M1947 trousers. His rank chevrons, Legion *écusson*, and two small re-enlistment chevrons (in yellow for NCOs, green for troops) are worn as a single array pinned to his left breast pocket. On the French M1950 TAP belt he wears a US compass pouch; and the paired canvas rifle cartridge pouches of the M1950 TAP equipment set, in place of the also-common US carbine pouches.

C4: Légionnaire 1ère classe, 13e Demi-Brigade de la Légion Étrangère; Dien Bien Phu, winter 1953-54 The 13e's beret is worn decorated with the single green diagonal braid marking this rank early in WWII. The M1943 US herringbone twill fatigue jacket – like the US 'M1941' and M1943 field jackets – was widely used early in the Indochina War, but was rare by the time this photo was taken. The olive sweater was an issue item; so increasingly was the M1951 steel helmet (which we have added to the original photographic subject), an ugly copy of the US M1. The M1947 fatigue trousers are worn with a French-made copy of the US pistol belt with British-type fittings.

DI: Légionnaire, Compagnie d'Instruction, 1er Régiment Étranger; Mascara, Algeria, summer 1957 From photographs of Norwegian Légionnaire 'Jean Eric Johanssen', in uniform and equipment typical of the early part of the Algerian War. During basic training, sketchily armed men of this unit were helicoptered into the hills of the nearby Djebel-el-Biar to intercept a reported ALN force; the subsequent action cost four French dead and six wounded. The 16-year-old 'Johanssen' was awarded the Croix de Valeur, and was thus one of the few trainees to report to his regiment already wearing a gallantry decoration (he would earn others while serving with the 2e REP). He was subsequently issued a MAT.49 submachine-gun, as illustrated (note security chain used on anti-guerrilla operations). The now-plentiful supply of MAT.49s had led to the tactical division of the Legion infantry section/squad into *voltigeurs* with SMGs forming the assault team – the proven men; and rifle-armed *pourvoyeurs* – the less experienced men who carried spare ammunition for the LMG fire team. He wears an M1946 *képi* with a khaki drill cover; M1947 fatigues, with a scarf in sub-unit recognition colour; French M1951 copies of US web leggings; and M1917 boots. The M1946 French brown leather equipment set now in widespread use comprised belt, suspenders, and various connectors and pouches (here, two for MAT.49 magazines) but no canteen carrier – the French M1950 is looped on in its canvas carrier. The pack is the 'all-arms musette M1950'.

RIGHT **Left sleeve insignia for a *caporal-chef*, 1960s: the Legion's grenade in gold on a midnight blue *écusson* with triple green edging, surmounted by one gold over two green rank chevrons, the small yellow chevron at the bottom marking one completed five-year enlistment.**

D2: Sergent, 1ère Compagnie Portée, 2e Régiment Étranger d'Infanterie; Djebel Beni-Smir, Algeria, December 1960 A figure typifying the légionnaire, on a typical operation, of the second half of the war. Attacking an ALN unit infiltrating the Moroccan frontier south of Ain-Sefra, six 'sticks' from the 1st Motorised Company, 2e REI were helicoptered onto Hill 1641 at 8.30am on 2 December 1960. Strong enemy forces held the LZ, however, driving off the helicopters with heavy damage after only six men, led by Sgt. Sanchez-Iglesias, had leapt out of the first. They held out alone and surrounded for nearly 12 hours; it took three companies with air support all day to fight their way up the hill. The ALN lost 63 dead and 16 prisoners from some 130 men, plus 60 weapons, 100 grenades, and some 10,000 rounds captured; the Legion, two dead and 11 wounded.

The bush hat appeared in *vert armée* at the end of the 1950s, fading rapidly in use; sand and green types continued to be worn side by side. From 1960 the green M1947 fatigues were replaced in all Legion combat units by camouflaged fatigues of similar cut except for external jacket skirt pockets – *tenue camouflée toutes armes* – in the same pattern as used for the paratroopers' *tenues de saut*. Note the buttoned-on rank tab of dark blue cloth with two gold stripes. Coloured recognition scarves were often worn at neck or shoulder on operations. The boots are French M1952 'rangers' with double-buckle ankle flaps, originally issued brown but by 1960 blackened. First line infantry units had increasingly received the M1950 *TAP* webbing set, here with a Rapco quick-release belt buckle and paired five-magazine pouches for the MAT.49. Stowed visibly on his M1951 all-arms *'bergram'* rucksack are the *djellaba* – a loose, hooded native robe of coarse wool, popular as an alternative to the issue greatcoat among Legion motorised units; and a camouflaged tent-quarter, sand-khaki on one side, and in a rather bright pattern of sand, red-brown and green on the other.

D3: Légionnaire, 1ère Compagnie Saharienne Portée de la Légion; Laghouat area, southern Algeria, c.1960 The field dress of the CSPLs, like their complex ceremonial uniforms, reflected both Legion and Compagnie Méhariste traditions. While M1947 fatigues and bush hat were standard issue in the 1950s – as were camouflaged fatigues and green beret in the early 1960s – this Saharan dress was also widely photographed. Motorcycle goggles were worn on the *képi*, which was covered in white or sand-khaki. The traditional desert *chèche* scarf (in pale sand-khaki, white usually being the mark of an officer) could be worn round the neck or, in sandstorms, rolled round the head as a turban. The sand-khaki smock – *gandourah* – was essentially unchanged since issued to Legion cavalry of the 1920s. The very loose seroual trousers were made in both sand-khaki drill, and in winter-weight khaki wool for wear with the M1946 battledress blouse (the latter type being essentially the M1923/35 *culotte des spahis*); taped ankle bands secured them above the *nail* sandals. The *djellaba* was also general issue. Photos show varied personal equipment worn in the field: M1950 *type TAP* webbing, this M1946 leather set, or even the traditional Saharan red/brown leather equipment with crossed pouch bandoliers. The rifle is the 7.5mm MAS.49/56, a self-loading weapon with a detachable ten-round magazine, which reached infantry units from 1957.

E1: Caporal, 3e Régiment Étranger d'Infanterie; winter guard dress, Algeria, c.1959 The basic M1946 *tenue de sortie* – walking-out dress, to which parade embellishments were added, and which remained in use until 1979 – was this khaki wool battledress worn over a khaki drill shirt and green Legion tie. The blouse had an open notched collar, two pleated pockets, and a waist band secured to the right with a buttoned half-belt; the anodised buttons were still essentially of the Legion's 1875 pattern. The trousers lacked visible leg pockets. The sleeve *écusson* (often seen with a regimental number in the 'bomb' before about 1962) and rank and re-enlistment chevrons were as described above. For walking-out the uniform was worn with the shoulderboards illustrated in Plate E2, and without a belt or gaiters, the trousers hanging loose. Additions/substitutions for *tenue de parade* were the Legion's blue sash and green and scarlet epaulettes (*ceinture* and *epaulettes de tradition*); belt and gaiters (of all contemporary types, and sometimes whitened for honour guards); and unit citation lanyards carried across to the top blouse button. The MAS.36 has its needle-bayonet fixed; when unfixed it fitted in the cylindrical housing beneath the barrel.

Sergeants and upwards wore the M1946 midnight blue and red *képi* uncovered, with the grenade badge on headgear and shoulderboards gold or silver, and gold or silver threads edging and barring the crescents of the parade epaulettes. Their *képi* bore a gold or silver lace false chinstrap, always worn up, with a second in lace-bordered black worn down for guard dress. Troops wore a white *képi*-cover, and their plain chinstrap was worn down for ceremonial. Depending on date and unit, *caporaux*- and *brigadiers-chef* wore the white-covered *képi*, with shoulderboard and sleeve grenade badges in yellow or white thread. The troops' *képi* of the Indochina period bore a red grenade, and those made later in Algeria a green grenade;

ABOVE **Borgo, Corsica, March 1963: *Caporal* Jim Worden, Bn. de M.3e REI (the regimental element not sent to Madagascar), wearing the all-arms camouflage fatigues – note buttoned rank tab on left breast, two green stripes on dark blue. (Courtesy Jim Worden)**

since they never wore the *képi* uncovered for any order of dress, it began to be made in plain sand-khaki with a white cover from about the mid-1960s, and in all-white material from the early 1970s.

In 1945 the 3e REI inherited the lineage of the wartime RMLE, and thus the US Presidential Citation ribbon on the right breast, and the double citation lanyard (see Plate C2). By the end of the Indochina campaign this had become the massive triple *fourragère* marking the regiment's unique record of 16 citations in Army orders. (The lanyards are in the colours of the Légion d'Honneur, Médaille Militaire, and Croix de Guerre 1914-18, with various complex 'olives' above the ferrules.) Personal awards here are the Croix de Valeur Militaire; Croix de Guerre TOE ('for Exterior Theatres of Operations'), replaced by the Croix de Valeur in 1956 due to the legal fiction that Algeria was part of France; the Indochina and Algeria campaign medals (the latter officially for

ABOVE **The cut-out grenade beret badge, here of 5e REI, worn c.1959-62; an example of unit variation of that period, here the silver grenade-and-horseshoe adopted by 2e REI in commemoration of the old Legion mule companies of mounted infantry; and the regulation un-numbered ringed grenade adopted as standard from c.1963.**

'Operations of Security and Maintenance of Order'); and a wound medal.

E2: Légionnaire 1ère classe, 5e Régiment Étranger d'Infanterie; summer walking-out dress, Algeria, c.1959 The M1946 summer/tropical equivalent of the battledress uniform, essentially unchanged today, was this khaki drill shirt and slacks worn with a narrow web belt copied from the US type. For evening the sleeves and collar have usually been worn fastened and the green tie added; for daytime, the sleeves rolled and the collar open; but this has not been a rigid distinction at all dates and stations. It was an 'old soldier's' fashion for the white-covered *képi* to acquire a slight upward roll to its peak. The shoulderboards, worn from about 1948 on both battledress and shirtsleeve uniforms, have a pocket-type uniform button, and three green inverted chevrons, inboard of the Legion grenade in green (gold or silver for NCOs). Regimental transfers were not unusual, and men who had seen action with a previous unit could add its badge to their left shoulderboard (miniatures were later substituted); this veteran of the 2e REP also wears his parachutist's qualification wings. The *fourragère* of the Croix de Guerre TOE marks the 5e REI's second citation in Army orders in 1950. Regimental badges were still sometimes pinned directly to the pocket at this date, rather than on a leather fob.

E3: Sous-officier, 2e Régiment Étranger de Cavalerie; Algeria, 1959 Before 1960 Legion armoured car crews lacked a convenient field headgear. Covered *képis* are worn in most photos; but there was also this khaki drill beret, a general service item widely used by French Union forces in Indochina (and also in Algeria by the 13e DBLE when khaki wool berets were no longer obtainable). It was usually seen without a badge; but in 1959 this non-regulation pattern, with a numbered grenade offset to the right, was observed in both the 1er and 2e RECs.

E4: Légionnaire, 3e Régiment Étranger d'Infanterie; Algeria, 1960 The green beret of the REPs was finally extended to the whole Legion in 1959-60. No suitable cap badge existed; this seven-flamed grenade was therefore procured at unit level (and never officially confirmed), in gold or silver with appropriate numbers, the latter replacing that shown in Plate E3 for the RECs. It was generally worn from 1960 until c.1963, when the universal pattern of an unnumbered grenade centred on an open circle was introduced – though there were a number of unit variations during these years. The issue of camouflage fatigues to non-airborne units from 1960 saw some initial use of various models of Airborne *tenues de saut in* REIs, RECs and CSPLs. The camouflaged netting face veil copied from the World War II British item was, and remains, popular as a field scarf.

F1: Commandant, 4e Régiment Étranger; Quartier Capitaine Danjou, Castelnaudary, France, 1980s The officer's *képi* throughout our period has been this black and red pattern, with infantry gold or cavalry silver lace – embroidered grenade, rank *galons*, vertical quarter-piping, false chinstrap, and on the crown an edging and a quatrefoil knot. *Adjudants* wear single lace of gold or silver with an interwoven red chevron pattern. Immediately after World War II various pre-war or wartime tunics were worn as officer's service dress; but from the late 1940s the M1946 battledress was adopted, worn with these stiff shoulderboards displaying rank, and the Legion's left sleeve *écusson*; the grenades on both were gold or silver. Officers and *adjudants* did not wear the blue sash or traditional epaulettes for parade. In Indochina a variety of khaki drill and white walking-out uniforms were individually acquired; a British-inspired four-pocket bush jacket with short sleeves and integral cloth belt was popular. In 1956 officers and warrant officers acquired this new four-pocket service tunic for walking-out; the *écusson* is pentagonal, with three green chevrons above a grenade, and worn now on the collars.

A

B

C

D

Insignia of higher formations worn on the right shoulder of service dress are a relatively recent feature of Legion ground troops' uniform. The only one generally worn in Algeria was (A), **Commandement Operationnel au Sahara, worn by the CSPLs – scarlet with pale blue Agades cross and bottom strip, white lettering and trim.** (B) **Forces Armées aux Antilles-Guyane, worn by 3e REI since 1973 – royal blue, yellow motifs, red trim.** (C) **31e Brigade, worn by 2e REI 1981-84 and by other Legion elements for the Beirut operation – pale blue, black motif, white stars, yellow waves, green/red/dark blue sidestripes.** (D) **6e DLB, currently worn by 1er REC, 2e REI, 6e REG – scarlet, silver gauntlet, green/gold wreath, gold trim.**

Shoulderboards, regimental badges, citation lanyards, decorations, and where appropriate the right shoulder patch of a higher formation, are applied. The matching khaki trousers have two 50mm dark brown stripes for officers, and a dark brown seam piping for warrant officers. Battledress continued to be worn for parades with troops; and photographs from the late 1940s to the early 1960s show occasional use of tunic collar patches instead of the left sleeve diamond on the BD blouse.

The BD parade dress passed out of use from c.1979, being replaced by the tunic. Note the dark green waistcoat particular to Legion officers, worn with a white shirt and dark green tie. A pale stone-coloured summer/tropical equivalent uniform lacks the trouser stripes (but is occasionally worn with the waistcoat in marginal weather). This major of the Legion's training unit wears the regimental badge on a fob of dark green, red-stitched leather from the right breast pocket; and the right shoulder patch of the 14e (formerly of the 4e) DLB to which it is operationally subordinated. Many personnel of non-airborne units are parachute-qualified.

(For more details of rank insignia see Elite 6, *French Foreign Legion Paratroops*, page 55.)

F2: Drum sergeant, Musique Principale; summer parade dress, Paris, Bastille Day, mid-1980s The shirtsleeve summer/tropical walking-out and parade uniform is worn in its fastened 'evening' format – bandsmen break a number of normal uniform rules. An obvious instance is that this NCO wears a white *képi* (of the all-white plasticised cloth construction, with a slightly countersunk crown, which appeared early in the 1970s), to give the marching band a uniform appearance, rather than the black and red of his rank. It was during the Algerian War that the Legion shirt (and the BD blouse) acquired the 16 decorative ironed creases on the breast, back and sleeves which are still seen today. Since about 1969 the 'rangers' boots have been made in black; white ladder-lacing has often been worn by bands and guards

A

B

C

D

E

F

Representative selection of regimental breast badges; there are many known detail variations, and introduction dates here refer only to the design: (A) **1er REI, 1951-55 – green\red, gold globe, silver grenade.** (B) **GALE 1950-55, 1er RE 1955 – white, red & green saltire, black eagle, green snake, gold trim.** (C) **2e REI c.1947-57 – green, gold dragon & trim, red grenade.** (D) **2e REI/RE 1957 – silver, green/red sidestripes.** (E) **3e REI local variation Indochina, late 1940s – gold, green/red panel, red tongue, black lettering.** (F) **3e REI late 1940s-early 1950s – silver, green/red & black panels, gold grenade & lettering.** (G) **3e REI early 1950s – gold, green/red panel, black lettering.** (H) **4e REI/RE – silver, red/green diagonals.**

G

H

of honour since Algerian days. Musicians wear a chevron in tricolour lace above their badges of rank; this lace also borders the drum banner, which bears the old motto *Legio Patria Nostra* – 'The Legion is Our Homeland'. The band is unique in wearing two breast badges – that of the 1er RE from the right pocket, and the Musique Principale from the left.

F3: Caporal-chef, 13e Demi-Brigade de la Légion Étrangère, tropical guard dress; Quartier Montclar, Djibouti, late 1980s Up to 100 nationalities are currently represented in the ranks of the Legion, including former African colonies. For guard dress this *capo-chef* wears a white *képi* (see comment under F2 – this rank currently wears the black/ red NCO *képi*) with gold lace false chinstrap and gold-trimmed functional second strap; and, in the extreme heat of Djibouti, parade appointments on a short-sleeved khaki drill shirt and shorts uniform which would normally be limited to *petit tenue de travail*. Dark green socks are turned down over polished black 'rangers'. The shirt has the traditional creases; NCO epaulettes are worn, with the sash, and the 13e's *fourragère* in the colours of the Médaille Militaire with appropriate 'olives' marking the regiment's four citations; the olive web belt of the M1974 equipment supports the FAMAS bayonet. On his right breast are parachute wings, and the fobbed regimental badge. Above the left pocket is the qualification badge of the Arta Beach Commando Training Centre (CECAP) in Djibouti. His medals are the Médaille d'Outre-Mer ('Overseas Medal' – the old Colonial Medal, renamed in 1962); and the National Defence Medal created in 1982.

G1: Légionnaire 1ère classe, 1er Régiment Étranger de Cavalerie, winter walking-out dress; Quartier Labouche, Orange, France, late 1980s Parading to receive his certificate of honourable discharge after five years' service, this senior private wears the standard winter *tenue de sortie* M1961. The beltless four-pocket khaki tunic and matching trousers were introduced for service and walking-out from that year, and are retained to this day (apart from a change of material in c.1968). It is worn with all appropriate insignia previously worn on the M1946 battledress *tenue de sortie*; for sergeants and up the sleeve *écusson* was replaced on the tunic by officer-style collar patches. Note sand-khaki shirt, green tie, low black laced shoes, and silver cavalry buttons. Above the regimental badge fobbed to his right breast pocket he wears parachute wings, and the round silver badge of the 1er REC's HQ Sqn.; above the left, the ribbon of the Overseas Medal; on the left shoulder is the REC's double lanyard marking six citations, in the colours of the Croix de Guerre 1914-18 and C de G T.OE. Above the rank chevron and *écusson* on his left sleeve is the dull orange ('bronze') wreathed swords badge of the *Certificat Militaire No.1* (CM1), a professional qualification for junior NCOs, required before promotion to sergeant. ('Silver' and 'gold' classes, termed *Brevet Militaire Professionel 1* and *2*, are required for promotion to *adjudant* and *adjudant-chef* respectively.) Invisible on his right shoulder is the patch of the 6th Light Armoured Division (6e DLB).

From c.1979 the M1946 battledress parade uniform (Plate E1) was rapidly replaced in all units by this service dress with the usual parade embellishments added, worn with the trousers bloused into polished boots and the web waistbelt with bayonet scabbard (see Elite 6, Plate 1). This was an unflattering and unpopular style. At the annual Camerone Day ceremonies at Aubagne in April 1991 a new parade uniform was unveiled by the 1er Régiment Étranger. In a light greyish khaki shade termed *terre de France*, it has a waist-length blouse with a wide open collar worn without insignia; a fly front; deep vertical pleats down each side of the chest, 'Norfolk jacket' style; no breast pockets; and single-button cuffs. All normal parade appointments are worn, unit badges being pinned directly to the right breast. The blouse is worn with matching plain trousers tucked into polished boots.

G2: Légionnaire 1ère classe, section LMG gunner, 1ère Compagnie, 2e Régiment Étranger d'Infanterie; Operation Épervier, Abéché, Chad, 1989 In the aftermath of the Algerian War the *tenue camouflée* was felt to be a provocative reminder of the mutinous paras; it was – officially – withdrawn from all troops in January 1963 in favour of the green M1947 outfit. New 'army green' fatigues, *treillis satin 300 M1964*, became standard issue in 1971, and have remained in service for some 25 years essentially unchanged. There were slight modifications in 1980; tightening, and shortening and elasticating of the waist, are routinely seen in elite corps such as the Legion, Marines and Airborne. Termed for the last decade or so *treillis F-1*, the uniform is readily identifiable by the two vertical chest pocket zippers. In Chad in the early 1970s these fatigues were worn with bush hats, and with full sleeve insignia – chevrons and *écussons*. The latter were later replaced by a small velcro patch on the left front edge to which reduced insignia are attached: troops and NCOs wear green and gold or silver diagonals corresponding to their sleeve chevrons, adjudants and officers horizontal gold or silver bars, with red centrestripes for the warrant ranks. Since the late 1970s name tags are velcro-fastened to the right breast; company-coloured shoulder scarves have been almost universal over the same period. The traditional *chêche* scarf remains popular for African postings, as an alternative to the camouflage net veil. Conventional field headgear is the green beret, or the M1978 F-1 helmet (see Plate H1). Since 1980 the standard personal weapon has been the 5.56mm FAMAS 'bullpup' rifle, and the following year the M1950 *TAP* webbing set was replaced by M1974 and M1979 items in synthetic material. The LMG gunner in our original photo wears belt, H-suspenders, a pair of double-layered three-magazine pouches, cleaning pouch, field dressing pouch (the old M1950 *type commando*), canteen carrier, bayonet scabbard, and a large NBC satchel on the left thigh – even though he carries the section's AA.52 light machine gun, the belt-fed 7.5mm weapon which replaced the FM.24/29 during the Algerian War.

G3: Légionnaire 1ère classe, platoon radio operator, 3e Compagnie, 13e Demi-Brigade de la Légion Étrangère; Djibouti, late 1980s A wide geographical range of possible deployment has preserved the Legion's traditional pragmatism in the choice of working dress. The 'all-arms' camouflaged version of the M1947 fatigues have been issued at need to troops on tropical postings, largely unchanged but often retailored. The *petit tenue de travail* – short-sleeved shirt (*chemisette*) and brief shorts in khaki drill and/or, from 1980, *vert armée* – have often been worn in the field instead of, or as here, mixed with the camouflaged fatigues. The tabard-like open-sided *chemise*

A

B

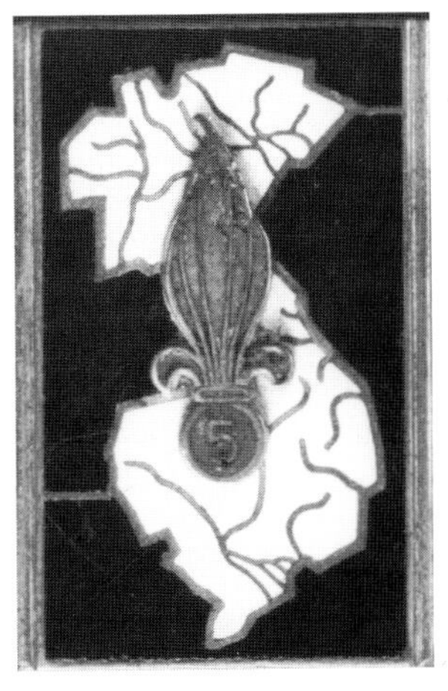

C

D

E

F

Regimental breast badges:
(A) **5^{e} REI – silver 1949-51, gold 1951-55, green outer, red inner borders.** (B) **5^{e} REI 1955-63 – black, white map, red flame, green bomb, gold trim.** (C) **5^{e} RMP 1963-83 – gold & black.** (D) **5^{e} RMP/RE 1983 – gold, shield green/red/over black, bomb blue.** (E) **6^{e} REI 1949-55 – silver, green/red diagonals.** (F) **13^{e} DBLE 1946 – gold, white panel, blue cross, green/red bars.** (G) **1er REC – silver, shield green/red/over blue, gold sunburst.** (H) **2^{e} REC 1947-61 – silver, shield green/red/over blue.**

G

H

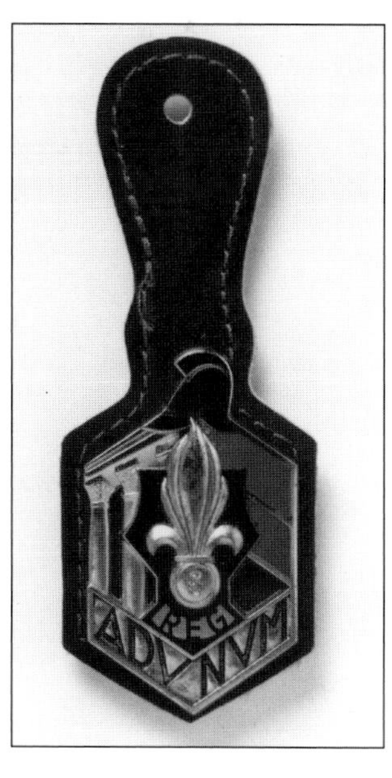

ABOVE **The gold badge of the 6e REG incorporates the old 6e REI's Baalbek ruins motif and motto, with the black helmet and cuirass of the Engineers. The fob is green with red stitching, as usual since the 1970s.**

echancrée of the alternative tenue GAO has been used in very hot postings, but is not generally popular. Photos show the 3e REI in Guiana wearing the KD *chemisette* combined with the green *treillis F-1* trousers. Berets and bush hats are worn depending on region and season. The multi-skilled motorised infantry element of the 13e DBLE – 3e Cie. – are distinguished by a yellow shoulder scarf. This platoon commander's radio operator, using the TRC-577 VHF/FM manpack transceiver, is equipped with the FAMAS rifle and full webbing, apart from the NBC satchel.

H1: Caporal, 6e Régiment Étranger de Génie; As Salman, Iraq, February 1991 Division Daguet initially deployed to the Gulf wearing temperate climate fatigues, later receiving new desert camouflage uniforms. Beneath the sand-coloured NBC suit this assault engineer wears fatigues cut like the green *treillis F-1*, but in sand-khaki with large irregular areas of chestnut brown and light grey drab – the same pattern as used for his helmet and body armour covers. The helmet is the M1978, the weapon the FAMAS, and the webbing the standard M1974/79 set in synthetic material complete with NBC kit; a rank patch is velcro'd to the body armour. Since the early 1980s there has been a general issue of short range radios to squad leaders in combat units, normally a 'handie-talkie' like this TR-PP-11B.

H2: Tireur d'élite, 3e Compagnie, 2e Régiment Étranger d'Infanterie; UNPROFOR, Bosnia, summer 1993 The French were prominent among the UN contingents in the experimental issue of modern super-heavy sniper rifles in addition to the standard 7.62mm FR F-2 squad sniper's weapon. These .50 cal. (12.7mm) bolt-action rifles, effective up to 3,000m range, are normally used for strategic sniping at high-value or 'hard' targets, area denial, ordnance clearance, etc. This marksman of the 2^{e} REI carries a McMillan M87(R); the Barrett M82 is issued to the specialist sniper platoon of 3^{e}/13^{e} DBLE in Africa. For UN service the new Spectra ballistic helmet is painted light blue; on the left and right shoulders respectively of the *treillis F-1* are brassards bearing the French tricolour and the UNO badge; and the body armour cover is in a new camouflage pattern of green and brown on light drab, clearly inspired by the desert scheme.

H3: Légionnaire 1ère classe, mortar platoon, Compagnie d'Éclairage et d'Appui, 2e Régiment Étranger d'Infanterie; IFOR, Bosnia, 1995 The armoured 2e REI's claim to deliver the Legion's heaviest punch is underlined by the strength of its Recce & Support Company (CEA), the largest in the French army; the fire support element has three eight-post Milan ATGW platoons, a battery of ten 20mm cannon, and two six-tube platoons of wheeled Hotchkiss-Brandt 120mm heavy mortars. This légionnaire carries a mortar round with incremental propellant charges fitted; it has a range of about 12km (seven miles plus). His fatigues and the covers for his Spectra helmet and body armour are the new *tenue camouflée* introduced progressively over the past two years. The French have steadily developed body armour since its first general issue in Beirut in 1982; this latest version has integral straps and D-rings for direct attachment of the personal equipment, and large front and back pockets for ceramic plates.

H4: Brigadier, 3e Escadron, 1er Régiment Étranger de Cavalerie; IFOR, Bosnia, February 1996 The new *tenue camouflée* includes this bad weather overjacket with a large hood, and a single downwards-buttoning 'epaulette' on the chest to take a rank slide. The latter, in use since the late 1980s, mimics the *patte d'epaule* of service dress with rank chevrons added at the bottom/outboard end. (These slides are also worn on shoulder straps in a new 'woolly pully' barracks dress.) Note the silver beret badge recalling that of 1959. This seven-flame Legion grenade offset to the right of an open circle, with a regimental number in the bomb, has reappeared at company/squadron level at various times since then, though never officially sanctioned. It was worn by 1er REC elements in Chad in the 1970s, and, since they took over the lineage of the 2^{e} REC in 1984, by the DLEM on Mayotte. In gold, with appropriate regimental numbers, it has been photographed worn by the 3^{e} REI in the early 1970s; and in 1994 by both 2^{e} REI and 13^{e} DBLE elements in Rwanda.

SELECT BIBLIOGRAPHY

Bartlett, Philippe, *Badges of the French Foreign Legion 1923-1989,* (private publication)

Debay, Yves, *The French Foreign Legion Today, Europa-Militaria No.10,* Windrow & Greene (1992)

Debay, Yves, *The French Foreign Legion in Action, Europa-Militaria No.11,* Windrow & Greene (1992)

Fall, Bernard, *Hell in a Very Small Place,* Lippincott (1967)

Fall, Bernard, *Street Without Joy,* Pall Mall Press (1961)

Heduy, Philippe, *La Guerre d'Indochine 1945-1954,* SPL, Paris (1981)

Horne, Alistair, *A Savage War of Peace: Algeria 1954-62,* Macmillan (1977)

O'Ballance, Edgar, *The Indo-China War 1945-54,* Faber & Faber (1964)

Porch, Douglas, *The French Foreign Legion,* Macmillan (1992)

Windrow, Martin, *Uniforms of the French Foreign Legion 1831-1981,* Blandford (1981)

Windrow, Martin, & Braby, Wayne, *French Foreign Legion Paratroops,* Osprey Elite No.6 (1985)

Képi Blanc magazine, *passim*

Lassus, Denis, 'Dien Bien Phu', in *Military Illustrated Past & Present* Nos.18, 20, 23, 27.

Notes sur les planches en colour

A1: Maréchal-des-logis, 1er Régiment Etranger de Cavalerie; Autriche, printemps 1945. Porte un uniforme presque exclusivement américain: uniforme de service en laine M1939 OD, chemise de laine OD, cravate OD légère, ceinture à pistolet et bretelles en toile à sangles, cartouchières SMG, jambieres, chaussures de service "flesh-out" (en cuir non tanné) M1943.
A2: Adjudant, Régiment de manche de la Légion Etrangère / Extrême-Orient ; Oran, le 10 février 1946). Ce régiment reçut des uniformes de combat britanniques en laine complets et du matériel en toile à sangles trois jours avant d'ambarquer sur le *Cameronia* pour l'Indochine. **A3**: Sergent, 2ème Régiment Etranger d'Infanterie; garnison en poste, Annam, v. 1950. Ce sous-officier orte le casque colonial français M1931, une chemise et un short britannique, le sanglage de base M1937 et les bottines tropicales françaises très appréciées en toile et caoutchouc.

B1: Légionnaire, 13ème Demi-Brigade de la Légion Etrangère; Cochinchine, 1948-50 qui porte un 'chino' de l'armée américaine et un short assorti. Il porte jambieres américains par dessus les brodequins français en cuir M1917. Il est équipé de la cartouchière américaine M1923, des bretelles M1936, d'un pansement et d'une sacoche à grenades à deux poches, plus une gourde britannique à bandoulière. **B2**: Soldat d'infanterie, 1950-54. Son poignard est une baïonnette Lebel M1886 raccourcie et il porte des grenades "offensives" françaises OF37. Son fusil est le MAS36 7,5mm, avec un chargeur fixe à cinq cartouches.Il porte le trellis M1947. **B3**: Mitrailleur de section, Infanterie de la Légion, Tonkin, 1950-54. Ce mitrailleur porte le casque américain M1 avec filet, le treillis M1947, les bottes M1917 et les chevillères en toile M1945, copiées sur le type britannique mais avec une seule bride et un système d'attache interne à languette et poche sur le bas.

C1: Lieutenant-Colonel Charton, RC.4, octobre 1950. Tout comme les barrettes de galon noir sur ses épaulettes, son calot porte les cinq galons de rang (or/argent/or/vide/argent/or). Il porte la chemise britannique tropicale de combat "vert jungle" et le pantalon en treillis khaki britannique. **C2**: Légionnaire, 2ème Compagnie, I/3ème Régiment Etranger d'Infanterie, Phu Tong Hoa, le 27 juillet 1948. Ce personnage porte la chemise de treillis khaki française M1946, le pantalon "chino" des surplus américains et la ceinture française d'avant-guerre. Le képi est le type M1946, avec une housse blanche à cordon. **C3**: Sergent, II/2è Régiment Etranger d'Infanterie, Laos, avril 1954. Il porte ses chevrons de rang, son écusson de Légion et deux petits chevrons de ré-engagé (jaunes pour les sous-officiers, verts pour les troupes) sur une seule rangée, agrafés à sa poche de poitrine gauche. **C4**: Légionnaire 1ère classe, 13ème Demi-Brigade de la Légion Etrangère, Dien Bien Phu, hiver 1953-54. Il porte son béret avec le vieux galon vert en diagonale indiquant le rang. Il a une veste de corvée américaine M1943 en tissu à chevrons sergé,

D1: Légionnaire, Compagnie d'Instruction, 1er Régiment Etranger, Mascara, Algérie, été 1957. Il porte un képi M1946 recouvert d'une housse khaki en coutil, un treillis M1947, une copie française M1951 du jambiere américain en toile à sangles, des bottes M1917 et du brellage français M1946 en cuir marron. **D2**: Sergent, 2e Régiment Etranger d'Infanterie, 1960. Les bottes sont des "rangers" françaises M1952 et il porte le sanglage TAP M1950. **D3**: Légionnaire, 1ère Compagnie Saharienne Portée de la Légion, région de Laghouat, sud de l'Algérie, v. 1960, sur son tenue cámouflée. Il porte des lunettes de motard sur son képi et la gandourah et serouals sable-khaki avec des nails.

E1: Caporal, 3e Régiment Etranger d'Infanterie, uniforme de garde d'hiver, Algérie, v. 1959. Il porte la tenue de sortie de base M1946 sur une chemise de coutil khaki et une cravatte verte de la Légion. **E2**: Légionnaire 1ère classe, 5e Régiment Etranger d'Infanterie, tenue de sortie d'été, Algérie, v. 1959. Equivalent M1946 pour l'été/les tropiques. **E3**: Sous-officier, 2e Régiment Etranger de Cavalerie, Algérie, 1959. Avant 1960, les équipages de blindés de la Légion n'avaient pas de couvre-chef pratique pour les campagnes. **E4**: Légionnaire, 3e Régiment Etranger d'Infanterie, Algérie 1960.
Le béret vert des REP fut finalement étendu à toute la Légion en 1959-60.

F1: Commandant, 4e Régiment Etranger, Quartier Capitaine Danjou, Castelnaudary, France, vers 1980. Ce commandant porte le badge du régiment sur un gousset de cuir vert foncé piqué de rouge sur la poche de poitrine droite. **F2**: Sergent tambour, Musique Principale, uniforme de parade d'été, Paris, 14 juillet, vers 1985. Il porte un képi blanc pour donner à la fanfare en parade l'apparence d'un uniforme plutôt que le képi noir et rouge correspondant à son rang. Les musiciens portent un chevron en galon tricolore au dessus de leur badge de rang. **F3**: Caporal-chef, 13e Demi-Brigade de la Légion Etrangère, uniforme tropical de garde, Quartier Montclar, Djibouti, fin des années 80. Comme uniforme de garde, il porte un képi blanc orné d'un galon doré, une fausse mentonnière et une seconde sangle fonctionnelle bordée d'or, une chemise à manches courtes en coutil khaki et un short d'uniforme.

G1: Légionnaire 1ère classe, 1er Régiment Etranger de Cavalerie, tenue de sortie d'hiver, Quartier Labouche, Orange, France, fin des années 80. Il porte la tenue de sortie d'hiver standard M1961. La tunique khaki à quatre poches et sans ceinture et le pantalon assorti sont encore utilisés aujourd'hui (mais avec un nouveau tissu depuis 1968 environ). **G2**: Légionnaire 1ère classe, 1ère Compagnie, 2e Régiment Etranger d'Infanterie. Opération Epervier, Abeche, Tchad, 1989. Il porte la tenue verte M1964, avec chêche et 'rangers', et la mitraillette AA.52 de la section.
G3: Légionnaire 1ère classe, opérateur radio de setion, 3e Compagnie, 13e Demi-Brigade de la Légion Etrangère; Djibouti, fin des années 80 en petite tenue de travail.

H1: Caporal, 6e Régiment Etranger du Génie, As Salman, Irak, février 1991. Sous la combinaison NBC couleur sable, il porte une tenue de travail coupée comme le treillis vert F-1 mais en khaki-sable camouflé en marron et grise claire. Le casque est le M1978, l'arme un FAMAS et le sanglage le standard M1974-79. **H2**: Tireur d'élite, 3e Compagnie, 2e Régiment Etranger d'Infanterie, UNPROFOR, Bosnie, été 1993. Ce tireur d'élite du 2e REI porte un McMillan M87(R). Sur l'épaule gauche et droite respectivement du treillis F-1 se trouve un brassard portant le tricolore français et le badge de l'ONU. **H3**: Légionnaire 1ère classe, section des mortiers, Compagnie d'Eclairage et d'Appui, 2e Régiment Etranger d'Infanterie, IFOR, Bosnie, 1995. Ce légionnaire en la nouvelle tenue camouflée porte de mortier lourd Hotchkiss-Brandt 120mm avec charges incrémentielles.
H4: Brigadier, 3e Escadron, 1er Régiment Etranger de Cavalerie, IFOR, Bosnie, février 1996. La tenue camouflée comporte cette sur-veste imperméable avec patte de rang.

Farbtafeln

A1: Marechal-des-logis, 1er Regiment Etranger de Cavalerie; Österreich, Frühjahr 1945. D Bekleidung des Soldaten besteht fast vollständig aus amerikanischen Beständen - M1939 OD Dienstanzug aus Wollstoff, OD-Wollhemd, helle OD-Krawatte, M1936 Pistolengurt ur Hosenträger, SMG-Patronentaschen, M1938 Leggings für nicht berittenen Einsatz und M194 "umgekehrte" Dienstschuhe. **A2:** Adjudant, Regiment de Marche de la Legion Etrangere / Fern Orient; Oran, 10. Februar 1946. An dieses Regiment wurden drei Tage vor der Abfahrt nac Indochina auf der *Cameronia* komplette Kampfuniformen britischer Herkunft aus Wollstoff ur Gurtbandausrüstungen ausgegeben. **A3:** Sergent, 2e Regiment Etranger d'Infanteri Garnisonsposten, Annam, ca. 1950. Dieser Unteroffizier trägt den französischen Kolonialhel M1931, ein britisches Hemd und kurze Hosen, eine vereinfachte Gurtausrüstung M1937 britische Herkunft sowie die populären französischen Halbstiefel aus Segeltuch und Gummi für die Trope

B1: Legionnaire, 13e Demi-Brigade de la Legion Etrangere; Cochinchina, 1948-50, in eine "Chino" der amerikanischen Armee und dazu passenden kurzen Hosen. Über den französische ledernen *brodequins* M1917 trägt er amerikanische Leggings. Der Soldat hat den amerikanische Patronengürtel M1923, Hosenträger des Modells M1936, eine Feldtasche und ein Granatenbeutel mit zwei Taschen bei sich. **B2:** Infanterist der Fremdenlegion; Tonkin, 1950-5 Bei seinem Dolch handelt es sich um ein gestutztes Bajonett der Machart Lebel M1886, und hat französische, "offensive" Sprenggranaten OF37 dabei. Sein Gewehr ist das 7,5mm MAS.3 mit einem feststehenden fünf-Schuß-Magazin. **B3:** Schütze für leichtes Maschinengeweh Infanterie der Fremdenlegion; Tonkin, 1950-54. Dieser Schütze trägt den amerikanischen M1 Helm mit Netz, den französischen Arbeitsanzug M1947, Stiefel des Modells M1917 und d kurzen Segeltuch-Gamaschen M1945, die der britischen Machart nachempfunden waren, jedoc nur einen Riemen hatten und am unteren Rand mit einer Zunge und Lasche befestigt wurden.

C1: Oberstleutnant Charton; RC, 4. Oktober 1950. Wie auf den schwarzen Litzenbalken auf seine Schulterklappen befinden sich auch auf der Mütze die fünf Rang-*galons*, bzw. Tressenbalke (Gold/Silber/Gold/Lücke/Silber/Gold). Er trägt das britische "dschungelgrüne" Tropenhemd un britische, khakifarbene Drillichhosen. **C2:** Legionnaire, 2. Kompanie, I/3e Regiment Etrange d'Infanterie; Phu Tong Hoa; 27. Juli 1948. Diese Figur trägt das französische, khakifarben Drillichhemd des Modells M1946, "Chino"-Hosen aus überzähligen Beständen der USA und de französischen Gürtel aus der Vorkriegszeit. Bei dem *kepi* handelt es sich um den Typ M1946 m einem weißen Bezug mit Durchziehband. **C3:** Sergent, II/2e Regiment Etranger d'Infanterie; Lao April 1954. Die Rangwinkel, Legion *ecusson* und zwei kleine Wiederanwerbungswinkel (b Unteroffizieren in gelb, bei den Mannschaften grün), werden als einzelne Abzeichenreihe an di linke Brusttasche geheftet getragen. **C4:** Legionnaire 1ere classe, 13e Demi-Brigade de la Legio Etrangere; Dien Bien Phu, im Winter 1953-54. Hier wird das Barett der 13e getragen, wobei d einzelne, grüne, diagonale Litzenkordel den Rang bezeichnet. Er trägt eine Arbeitsjacke au Köperstoff im Fischgrätmuster der Machart M1943 amerikanischer Herkunft.

D1: Legionnaire, Compagnie d'Instruction, 1er Regiment Etranger; Mascara, Algerien, im Somme 1957. Er trägt ein *kepi* des Modells M1946 mit einem Bezug aus khakifarbenem Drillich, de Arbeitsanzug M1947, französische M1951-Kopien der amerikanischen Gurtband-Legging M1917-Stiefel und eine französische Ausrüstung M1946 aus braunem Leder. **D2:** Sergent, 1er Compagnie Portee, 2e Regiment Etranger d'Infanterie; Djebel Beni-Smir, Algerien, im Dezembe 1960. Bei den Stiefeln handelt es sich um die französischen "Ranger" des Modells M1952. E trägt die Gurtbandausrüstung M1950 TAP. **D3:** Legionnaire, 1ere Compagnie Saharienne Porte de la Legion; Laghouat-Gebiet, Südalgerien, ca. 1960.

E1: Caporal, 3e Regiment Etranger d'Infanterie; Wachanzug für den Winter, Algerien, ca. 1959. E trägt den einfachen *tenue de sortie* - also Ausgehanzug - M1946, einen khakifarbene Kampfanzug aus Wollstoff, der über ein khakifarbenes Drillichhemd und eine grüne Krawatte de Fremdenlegion getragen wurde. **E2:** Legionnaire 1ere classe, 5e Regiment Etranger d'Infanteri Ausgehanzug für den Sommer, Algerien, ca. 1959. Bei dieser Aufmachung handelt es sich um da Gegenstück zur Kampfuniform für den Sommer bzw. die Tropen M1946. **E3:** Sous-officier, 2 Regiment Etranger de Cavalerie; Algerien, 1959. Vor 1960 fehlte es den Mannschaften de Panzerfahrzeuge der Fremdenlegion an einer geeigneten Kopfbedeckung im Feld. **E4** Legionnaire, 3e Regiment Etranger; Quartier Capitaine Danjou, Castelnaudary, Frankreich, in de 80er Jahren. Dieser Major trägt das Regimentsabzeichen an einer Kordel aus dunkelgrünem, rc abgestepptem Leder an der rechten Brusttasche.

F2: Tambour-Feldwebel, Musique Principale; Sommerparadeanzug, Paris, Nationalfeiertag 14 Juli, Mitte der 80er Jahre. Um der Militärkapelle ein einheitliches Äußeres zu verleihen, trägt e ein weißes *kepi* anstatt des schwarz-roten, das seinem Rang entspräche. Die Musiker trage einen Winkel aus Trikolore-Litze über ihrem Rangabzeichen. **F3:** Caporal-chef, 13e Demi-Brigad de la Legion Etrangere, Wachanzug für die Tropen; Quartier Montclar, Djibouti, Ende der 80e Jahre. Zur Wache trägt er ein weißes *kepi* mit einem falschen Kinnriemen aus Goldlitze und einer goldfarben eingefaßten, funktionellen, zweiten Riemen, ein kurzärmeliges, khakifarbene Drillichhemd und kurze Hosen.

G1: Legionnaire 1ere classe, 1er Regiment Etranger de Cavalerie, Ausgehanzug für den Winter Quartier Labouche, Orange, Frankreich, Ende der 80er Jahre. Der Legionär trägt de standardmäßigen *tenue de sortie* M1961 für den Winter. Der gürtellose, khakifarbene Waffenroc mit vier Taschen und dazu passenden Hosen wurde bis zum heutigen Tag beibehalten (abgesehe von einer Änderung des Materials um 1968). **G2:** Legionnaire 1ere classe, Schütze für leichte Maschinengewehr, 1ere Compagnie, 2e Regiment Etranger d'Infanterie; Operation Epervie Abeche, Tschad, 1989, in der grünen Uniform M1947. Er hat das leichte Maschinengewehr AA.5 der Abteilung bei sich. **G3:** Legionnaire 1ere classe, Funker des Zugs, 3e Compagnie, 13e Demi Brigade de la Legion Etrangere; Djibouti, Ende der 80er Jahre, im Arbeitsanzug des Modell M1947 - *petit tenue de travail.*

H1: Caporal, 6e Regiment Etranger de Genie; As Salman, Irak, Februar 1991. Unter dem sand farbenen NBC-Anzug trägt dieses Mitglied der Genietruppe einen Arbeitsanzug im Schnitt de grünen *treillis F-1*, jedoch sand-/khakifarben. Bei dem Helm handelt es sich um M1978, die Waff ist das FAMAS, und das Textilkoppel entspricht der standardmäßigen Ausführung M1974/79. **H2** Tireur d'elite, 3e Compagnie, 2e Regiment Etranger d'Infanterie; UNPROFOR, Bosnien, im Somme 1993. Dieser Scharfschütze des 2e REI hat ein McMillan M87(R). Auf der rechten und linke Schulter des *treillis F-1* sind jeweils das französische Trikolore-Abzeichen und das UNO-Emblen zu sehen. **H3:** Legionnaire 1ere classe, Minenwerferzug, Compagnie d'Eclairage et d'Appui, 2e Regiment Etranger d'Infanterie; IFOR, Bosnien, 1995. Dieser Legionär trägt eine Runde Hotchkiss Brandt 120mm schwere Mörser mit zunehmender Treibladung. **H4:** Brigadier, 3e Escadron, 1e Regiment Etranger de Cavalerie; IFOR, Bosnien, im Februar 1996. Zum neuen *tenue camoufle* gehört diese Überjacke für schlechtes Wetter.